THE THEATRE OF IMAGES

THE THEATRE OF IMAGES

PANDERING TO THE MASSES:
A MISREPRESENTATION
RICHARD FOREMAN

A LETTER FOR QUEEN VICTORIA
ROBERT WILSON

THE RED HORSE ANIMATION
LEE BREUER

EDITED WITH INTRODUCTORY ESSAYS BY BONNIE MARRANCA

DRAMA BOOK SPECIALISTS (PUBLISHERS)
NEW YORK

Library of Congress Cataloging in Publication Data

The Theatre of images.

  CONTENTS: Foreman, R. Pandering to the masses.—Breuer, L. The red horse animation.—Wilson, R. A letter for Queen Victoria.

  1. American drama—20th century. I. Marranca, Bonnie. II. Foreman, Richard, 1937-   Pandering to the masses. 1977. III. Breuer, Lee. The red horse animation. 1977. IV. Wilson, Robert, 1928-   A letter for Queen Victoria. 1977.
PS634.T515   812'.5'408   77-23205
ISBN 0-910482-83-7
ISBN 0-910482-89-6 pbk.

Book design: Linda Readerman
Typography: A&S Graphics, Wantagh, New York
Text printing: Noble Offset Printers, New York City
Color printing: Rapoport Printing Corp., New York City

Printed in the United States of America

To My Mother
Who always encouraged me

B.G.M.

I wish to thank Julie Hymen and Cynthia Lubar of the Byrd Hoffman Foundation for their assistance in preparing the completed script of A Letter for Queen Victoria; *Mimi Johnson and Jane Yockel of Performing Artservices, Inc. for kindly making available to me their files for research purposes; Barbara Skluth for her helpful suggestions; Linda Readerman of Drama Book Specialists (Publishers) for patiently accepting the manuscript, literally, bit by bit. My warmest appreciation to my husband, Gautam Dasgupta, for his useful comments and for the endless conversations from which many of the ideas in my introductory essays first began to emerge.*

Bonnie Marranca

What is the answer?

————————————————————

In that case, what is the question?
Gertrude Stein

The best answers are those that destroy the question.
Susan Sontag

CONTENTS

INTRODUCTION

In the last dozen years the American avant-garde theatre has emerged as a dynamic voice in the international arts scene. From its crude beginnings in out-of-the-way lofts, churches, private clubs and renovated spaces, it has become for many the liveliest, most creative center of theatrical activity in the West. This is due partly to the help of grant monies, but primarily to the emergence of a number of highly imaginative and gifted theatre artists.

Experimental groups of the sixties and early seventies broke down traditional parameters of theatrical experience by introducing new approaches to acting, playwriting and the creation of theatrical environments; they reorganized audience and performing space relationships, and eliminated dialogue from drama. Collaborative creation became the rule.

Value came increasingly to be placed on performance with the result that the new theatre never became a literary theatre, but one dominated by images—visual and aural. This is the single most important feature of contemporary American theatre, and it is characteristic of the works of groups *and* playwrights. As early as eight years ago Richard Kostelanetz pointed out the non-literary character of the American theatre when he wrote in *The Theatre of Mixed Means:*

> . . .the new theatre contributes to the contemporary cultural revolt against the pre-dominance of the word; for it is definitely a theatre for a post-literate (which is not the same as illiterate) age. . . .[1]

[1]Richard Kostelanetz, *Theatre of Mixed Means* (N.Y.: Dial Press, 1968), p. 33.

If this theatre refused to believe in the supremacy of language as a critique of reality, it offered a multiplicity of images in its place. Kostelanetz's McLuhanesque statement clarifies the direction that the American theatre has steadily followed since the Happenings. It has now culminated in a Theatre of Images—the generic term I have chosen to define a particular style of the American avant-garde which is represented here by Richard Foreman (Ontological-Hysteric Theater), Robert Wilson (Byrd Hoffman School of Byrds) and Lee Breuer (Mabou Mines).

The works of Foreman, Wilson and Breuer represent the climactic point of a movement in the American avant-garde that extends from The Living Theatre, The Open Theater, The Performance Group, The Manhattan Project and The Iowa Theatre Lab, to the "show and tell" styles of political groups like El Teatro Campesino, The San Francisco Mime Troupe and The Bread and Puppet Theatre. (And it is continued in the current proliferation of art-performances.) Today it is demonstrated in the image-oriented Structuralist Workshop of Michael Kirby and in the works of younger artists: *Sakonnet Point* by Spalding Gray and Elizabeth LeCompte; the "spectacles" of Stuart Sherman. All of the productions and groups mentioned above exclude dialogue or use words minimally in favor of aural, visual and verbal imagery that calls for alternative modes of perception on the part of the audience. This break from a theatrical structure founded on dialogue marks a watershed in the history of American theatre, a *rite de passage*.

The intention of this Introduction is to demonstrate the significance of this Theatre of Images, its derivation from theatrical and non-theatrical sources, its distinctively American roots in the avant-garde, its embodiment of a certain contemporary sensibility and its impact on audiences.

This essay, which will first isolate characteristics of the Theatre of Images and then deal at length with the specific pieces published here, will perhaps suggest an attitude to bring to this theatre. Hopefully, it will also offer helpful, new tools of analysis—an alternative critical vocabulary—with which to view contemporary theatre.

The absence of dialogue leads to the predominance of the stage picture in the Theatre of Images. This voids all considerations of theatre as it is conventionally understood in terms of plot, character, setting, language and movement. Actors do not create "roles." They function instead as media through which the playwright expresses his ideas; they serve as icons and images. Text is merely a pretext—a scenario.

The texts as published here (less so in the case of *The Red Horse Animation* which offers a comic book as a textual alternative) remain incomplete documents of a theatre that must be seen to be understood; one cannot talk about the works of Foreman, Wilson and Breuer without talking about their productions. Attending a theatrical performance is always an experience apart from reading a dramatic text; but a playscript *does* generally stand on its own merits as a pleasurable experience, indicating what it is about and usually giving a clue as to how it is staged. Conversely, reading Wilson's *A Letter for Queen Victoria* can be frustrating for readers attuned to theme, character, story, genre and logical language structure. There is scarcely a clue to its presentation in a script composed of bits and pieces of overheard conversations, television and films. Similarly, in Foreman's work, which insists on demonstrating what the words say (in Wittgensteinian-styled language games), to read the text alone is to lose the sensual delight and intellectual exchange of his theatre. And *The Red Horse Animation* is not a play at all.

Just as the Happenings had no immediate theatrical antecedents, the Theatre of Images, though not quite so renegade, has developed aesthetically from numerous non-theatrical roots. This is not to say that this movement disregards theatrical practices of the past: It is the application of them that makes the difference. More directly, the avant-garde must use the past in order to create a dialogue with it.

Foreman's work shows the influence (and the radicalization) of Brechtian technique; Breuer has acknowledged his attempt to synthesize the acting theories of Stanislavsky, Brecht and Grotowski; the productions of Wilson descend from Wagner. However, in their work, spatial, temporal and linguistic concepts are non-theatrically conditioned. Extra-theatrical influences have had a more formative impact. Cagean aesthetics, new dance, popular cultural forms, painting, sculpture and the cinema are important forces that have shaped the Theatre of Images. It is also logical that America, a highly technological society dominated by aural and visual stimuli, should produce this kind of theatre created, almost exclusively, by a generation of artists who grew up with television and movies.

The proliferation of images, ideas and forms available to the artist in such a culture leads to a crisis in the artist's choice of creative materials, and in his relationship to the art object. It is not surprising, then, that all of the pieces collected here are metatheatrical: They are about the making of art. In *Pandering to the Masses: A Misrepresentation* Foreman speaks directly to the audience (on tape) concerning the "correct" interpretation of events *as they occur.* The actors relate the formal "Outline" of the production at intervals in *Red Horse.* The result is a high degree of focus on process. How one sees is as important as what one sees.

This focus on process—the producedness, or seams-showing quality of a work—is an attempt to make the audience more conscious of events in the theatre than they are accustomed to. It is the idea of *being there* in the theatre that is the impulse behind Foreman's emphasis on immediacy in the relationship of the audience to the theatrical event.

The importance given to consciousness in the Theatre of Images is also manifest in its use of individual psychologies: Foreman in his psychology of art; Wilson in his collaboration with Christopher Knowles, an autistic teenager whose personal psychology is used as creative material (not as a psychology of the disturbed); and in Breuer's interest in motivational acting. In *Pandering,* life and theatre merge as Foreman incorporates his thoughts into the written text. In *Queen Victoria,* Wilson adapts, if only partially, autistic behavior as an alternative, positive mode of perceiving life. Through Breuer's use of interior monologue, the consciousness of the Horse is explored in *Red Horse.*

Each artist refrains from developing character in a predictable, narrative framework which would evoke conditioned patterns of intellectual and emotional response. Like all modernist experiments, which necessarily suggest a new way to perceive familiar objects and events, their works agitate for radical, alternative modes of perception.

In the Theatre of Images the painterly and sculptural qualities of performance are stressed, transforming this theatre into a spatially-dominated one activated by sense impressions, as opposed to a time-dominated one ruled by linear narrative. Like modern painting, the Theatre of Images is timeless (*Queen Victoria* could easily be expanded or contracted), abstract and presentational (in *Red Horse,* images are both abstract and anthropomorphic), often static (the principle of duration rules the work of

Foreman and Wilson); frequently the stage picture is framed two-dimensionally (in *Pandering* the actors are often poised in frontal positions). Objects are dematerialized, functioning in their natural rhythmic context. The body of the actor is malleable and pictorial—like the three actors who form multiple images of an Arabian steed lying *on* the performing space *(Red Horse)*. It is the flattening of the image (stage picture) that characterizes the Theatre of Images, just as it does modern painting.

If the acting is pictorial, it is also nonvirtuosic, an inheritance from the new dance which emphasizes natural movement. This is an aesthetic quality of the particular branch of the avant-garde dealt with here. What I wish to suggest is that the Theatre of Images in performance demonstrates a radical refunctioning of naturalism. It uses the performer's natural, individual movements as a starting point in production. Of the artists featured in this anthology, Foreman is the most thoroughly naturalistic. He allows performers (untrained) a personal freedom of expression while at the same time making them appear highly stylized in slow-motion, speeded-up, noninflectional patterns of speech or movement. He also pays a great deal of attention to actual situation and detail and the factor of time. Foreman's work is stylized yet naturalistic as are Alain Resnais' *Last Year at Marienbad* and Marguerite Duras' *India Song*.

The naturalism of nontraditional theatre is a curious phenomenon but one worth paying attention to because of its prevalence and diversity; it is also quite a paradox to admit that the avant-garde, in 1976, is naturalistic. In addition to being characteristic of the scripts printed here, it has shown itself in the production of David Gaard's *The Marilyn Project* directed last year by Richard Schechner, in Scott Burton's recent art-performance *Pair Behavior Tableaux,* as well as in Peter Handke's play without words, *My Foot My Tutor.* In these works there is a high degree of stylization by performers who "naturally" engage in an activity which is presented pictorially.

Perhaps that is why, in the Theatre of Images, tableau is so often the chief unit of composition. Tableau, in fact, has been a dominant structure in the work of twentieth-century innovators: the Cubists, Gertrude Stein, Bertolt Brecht, Jean-Luc Godard, Alain Robbe-Grillet, Philip Glass, to name a few. It is evident in the work of Foreman, Wilson and Breuer as well. Tableau has the multiple function of compelling the spectator to analyze its specific placement in the artistic framework, stopping time by throwing a scene into relief, expanding time and framing scenes. In *Pandering,* the tableaux function as objects in a cubist space, very often confusing perception by the intrusion of a single kinetic element. The cinematic "cuts" of *Red Horse* frequently focus the actors in close-up; "frames" are duplicated in the actual comic book documentation of the performance.

The stillness of tableau sequences suspends time, causing the eye to focus on an image, and slows down the process of input. This increases the critical activity of the mind. For Foreman it represents the ideal moment to impart taped directives to the audience; it also regulates the dialectical interplay of word and image.

Neither time nor space are bound by conventional law. Time is slowed-down, speeded-up—experienced as duration. It is never clocked time. Likewise, spatial readjustment is frequent in all of the pieces published here. *Red Horse* is played in multiple viewing perspectives: The actors perform both lying on the floor and standing on it, and up against a back wall of the performing space. *Pandering* alternates easily from flat perspective to linear perspective; the actors continually rearrange the drapes and flats of the set during performance. In *Queen Victoria* space is divided, cut apart and blackened—usually by means of light—leaving the actors to serve as images or silhouettes in a surreal landscape.

If time and space are dysynchronous in the Theatre of Images, so is language broken apart and disordered. The language of *Queen Victoria* is "throwaway," devoid of content. In *Red Horse* choral narrative is correlated with the image in space as interior monologue substitutes for dialogue. *Pandering* is ruled by the distributive principle of sound: Actors speak parts of sentences which are completed either by other actors or Foreman's voice on tape.

Sound is used sculpturally, just as the actors are. Aural tableaux complement or work dialectically with visual tableaux. In *Pandering* the audience, surrounded by stereo speakers, is bombarded with sound. Sound and visual images dominate in performance in an attempt to expand normal capabilities for experiencing sense stimuli. Because of the sophisticated sound equipment used in the productions of Foreman, Wilson and Breuer it is reasonable to conclude that the Theatre of Images would not exist without the benefit of advanced technology. Perhaps experiments with holography may lead in the future to a theatre of total images and recorded sound.

The significance of the Theatre of Images is its expansion of the audience's capacity to perceive. It is a theatre devoted to the creation of a new stage language, a visual grammar "written" in sophisticated perceptual codes. To break these codes is to enter the refined, sensual worlds this theatre offers.

Here, then, are three examples of the best of the American avant-garde theatre: works which break down the parameters of human experience which we have too hastily accepted.

BONNIE MARRANCA
NEW YORK CITY, 1976

PANDERING TO THE MASSES: A MISREPRESENTATION

RICHARD FOREMAN

RICHARD FORE/AAN:
THE ONTOLOGICAL-HYSTERIC THEATER

Richard Foreman is a philosopher-playwright, an anomaly in the American theatre which has never been a philosophical one. In his work with the Ontological-Hysteric Theater Foreman takes as his point of departure the philosophical, psychological and aesthetic writings of modern thinkers—in short, the Western epistemological tradition. Here is an avant-gardist who is also a classicist. Foreman both challenges and respects the foundations of contemporary thought.

The Ontological-Hysteric Theater dramatizes thinking processes in a highly complex series of images. In *Pandering to the Masses: A Misrepresentation* Foreman creates a reality that reflects his own being-in-the-world, demonstrating in the process a rigorous, alternative manner of focusing on familiar, everyday events. *Pandering,* then, functions on two levels. The subjective nature of the play co-exists with the objective relationship of the audience to the theatre event (the central focus of the production).

Pandering appears, on the surface, to have dialogue. However, it is not dialogue as understood in usual theatre terms. In Foreman's conception of dramaturgy the spoken language is not only nondiscursive but flattened out through the elimination of inflectional patterns. This flatness is duplicated in the performances of the actors, whose attention to detail and emphasis on natural rhythms of movement and speech produce an extreme naturalism. Speech is disconnected from the speaker by means of

3

interruptive devices such as the tape-recorded VOICE (of Foreman) and the voices of the other actors (live and on tape). Instead of engaging in conversational dialogue with one another, the actors, who function as "speakers," serve as the media of Foreman's ideas; they are "demonstrators."

The Ontological-Hysteric Theater is a theatre of illustrations in which pictures, continually interrelating with words, replace dialogue. Language exists in the domain of the phenomenological, used merely to indicate a reality in space; space becomes semantic. Foreman is Husserl's "meditating phenomenologist" who, in *Pandering,* meditates on his own and others' attitudes towards art.

In *Pandering* Foreman's focal point is the dual subject of the creation of art and the audience's perception of it. He challenges the popular notion of the acquisition of knowledge about an art object in a dialectical framework that is highly personal.

In performance the actors function cubistically, as multiple facets of Foreman's personality, varying degrees of his subconscious. They also reflect his observations while writing *Pandering.* This accounts for the documentary aspect of the play which, on one level, is a record of Foreman's thoughts while he was in the actual process of creating the play.

The actors, then, serve as blank faces (negative physiognomies) on which Foreman sketches aspects of his "being-in-the-world"; they are representatives of figures of his inner life, playing out the contradictions of his life as a social being. The writer MAX is the pivotal figure of the play; he embodies Foreman, the creative artist. RHODA is the thematic representative of sexuality. Together they manifest the interplay of the intellectual and the sensual which dominates the play. In this display of first-person consciousness Foreman offers the purest form of psychodrama viewed up to this time in the American theatre. One scene, in particular, illustrates the personal factor of *Pandering.* Toward the end of the production a man on a bicycle peddles furiously (he represents the energy force of Knowledge) while firing shots at RHODA. The VOICE offers a word—"IKON"—to explain the psychological maneuver which follows this scene. Then, the VOICE continues:

> He [MAX] inhabits that word. That means to
> celebrate finally he thinks about his face as being
> her face so he thinks about his person as being her
> person finally, and worships it finally, and reads it
> finally like a wonderful book.

RHODA is a substitute for MAX who, in actuality, is Richard Foreman. RHODA functions as both icon and idea.

On a second level, Foreman carries on a dialogue with the history of Western thought in which he attacks conventional modes of acquiring knowledge; in particular, knowledge gained in the perception of an event. *Pandering* is as much a play about Foreman as it is about the audience. In the staging of it Foreman sits in the first row of audience bleachers. From this vantage point he operates the tape system for the production (with himself as the taped VOICE that dominates the work) while also identifying himself as an audience member by his presence among the spectators. From this dual perspective of author-spectator the VOICE on tape comments on the kinds of responses elicited by the "old theatre." At one point in the production the VOICE declares:

> The old theater would prove to you that MAX is
> dancing the way that he is dancing, by which is
> meant, his motives, proven real and genuine, and
> you are convinced in a way appropriate to the
> theater.

Interestingly, *Pandering* bears a striking resemblance to Peter Handke's *Sprechstücke* which eliminate dramatic dialogue, employ "speakers" or "demonstrators" rather than characters, construct a dialogue between stage and audience, and debate with conventional theatre. Likewise, Foreman's work can be looked upon as "autonomous prologues to old plays" (Handke's phrase). And *Pandering to the Masses: A Misrepresentation* is as ironic a title as Handke's *Offending the Audience*—both are the "speak-ins" *(Sprechstücke)* of their authors.

Pandering is presented to the audience in the form of a "lecture-demonstration." Verbal and visual images accompany Foreman's running commentary. For example, the VOICE remarks on the occasion of one of RHODA'S adventures:

> . . . every experience through perhaps peripheral to
> primary revelation of knowledge, friendship, and
> inventiveness, still every experience can be a learn-
> ing experience if allowed to take its place in the
> mapping process of one's private adventure and
> spatial self orientation.

Projected slides ("legends"), which one may consider a more sophisticated variation of flash cards than those used by teachers in classrooms, carry content, which corresponds to or contradicts the image on stage, or describe an image that has already appeared or is about to appear ("He goes to the wall / finds two peepholes"). At the opening of the piece the VOICE virtually insults the audience's intelligence in a "lecture" that declares:

> You understand nothing. MAX regretfully concludes
> that you who watch and wait have unfortunately
> proven through your actions and reactions that
> certain subtle, exact, specific and necessary areas
> of understanding are not available to your—

The audience is left to fill in the blank.

Frequent "recapitulations" in the text reflect Foreman's didacticism. Yet they also have other functions. They serve as a flashback technique, or to further the action of the production by the interaction between Foreman and the actor on stage; often, they reinforce the memory of past events or clarify certain points of the text. In one instance, a "recapitulation" is calculated to make the audience reflect on the associative mode of preception. Foreman chides the audience, "Do you think using the associative method? Everybody does, you know." Like Gertrude Stein, whose writings, he has admitted, have been a major influence on his aesthetic theories, Foreman contrives to destroy associational emotion in the experience of a work of art. More significant, however, is Foreman's ability to create in his work what Stein referred to as the "actual present." *Pandering* exists in a dual framework: as the actual diary—the personal notes—of the playwright while he was writing the play over a certain period of time, and as a complete play unfolding in performance time. The past and present merge in the actuality of the performance.

In another allusion to a major Steinian concern, the VOICE directly confronts the issue of which image on stage takes precedence over another in the sequence of events:

> You can either watch MAX writing it, or you can
> watch what he is writing. But you can only watch
> what he is writing after he is writing it, and in that
> case your expectations are in a different direction,
> are they not?

Similarly, in a lecture entitled "Plays" (1934) Gertrude Stein observed that the audience is always ahead of or behind a play on stage, never exactly "with it."[1]

---

[1]*Gertrude Stein: Writings and Lectures 1909-1945*, ed. Patricia Meyerowitz (Baltimore, Maryland: Penguin Books, 1971), p. 59.

Bob Fleischner, Gail Conrad, John Erdman, Suzanne Oshry, Kate Manheim.   Photo © Babette Mangolte.

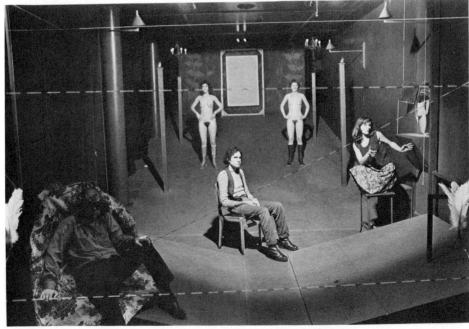

Bob Fleischner, Aline Lillie Mayer, John Erdman, Sheila McLaughlin, Kate Manheim.
Photo © Babette Mangolte.

To both Stein and Foreman it is the *conscious* act of experiencing events at a certain time and place that is important. In *Pandering* Foreman seeks the triumph of the conscious over the unconscious.

Pandering is a consciousness-raising piece—a teaching play—whose goal is to make audience members aware of their moment-by-moment existence in the theatre. For this reason alienating devices obtrude throughout the production. Foreman continually breaks down the production into smaller and smaller units or frames. He imposes a play, *Fear,* within the play. Many of the actors' lines are prerecorded on tape in Foreman's VOICE which interrupts them; the actors interrupt each other's speeches when each word in a sentence is spoken by a different person. Buzzers, loud thuds and music focused directionally by four stereo speakers which surround the audience, punctuate the actors' words. Scene titles, when they are used, break the flow of the production.

Foreman's use of these "alienation effects," more directly, his conception of a play as a "teaching play," reflects his Brechtianism. However, he is formalistically more radical than Brecht. Foreman breaks up his scenes into smaller and smaller units; Brecht divided his epic structures into unified scenic elements. Foreman is a minimalist concerned with instantaneous perception; Brecht's view was epic and historical, concerned not so much with momentary perception but with critical thinking which would lead to political activism outside the theatre. In Brecht's productions the actor "commented" on or "quoted" a past action; *Pandering* strives to create a continuous present even as it treats events of the past, i.e., Foreman's thoughts while writing it. Furthermore, though both artists devised dialectical theatres of illustration, Foreman has gone further than Brecht by moving the dialogue from its fixed position in a play on stage to a dialogue (metaphorical) between stage and audience. In this way, the dialectical aspect does not remain solely in the framework of the play on stage but occurs directly in the relationship of the audience to the production *in process.* (Handke has also accomplished this in his *Sprechstücke.*) Foreman always demonstrates *how* the play works.

Pandering emphasizes its producedness, i.e., the interconnection of its parts. This focus on structure necessarily compels the audience to scan it for minute alterations. By calling attention to itself—how it works—it stimulates the audience's powers of perception. The Ontological-Hysteric Theater is radically opposed to the traditional theatre (what Brecht called the "culinary" theatre) which feeds information to the audience by suggesting the "proper" emotions and responses to stage events. In Foreman's theatre there are no touchstones, no recognizable pegs on which to hang conditioned responses or ideas. The world of the play, while not duplicating reality, suggests a way to view life in the real world. Through Foreman's reduction of his personal life to a series of images one is led to perceive things as they are in themselves—not by learned patterns of perception but in an unconditioned way. Observation supersedes memory.

Foreman's emphasis on change, conscious response, the present moment, his use of "recapitulations" and taped directives for viewing *Pandering* force the audience to be aware of the making-of-theatre. Thus, the process of *Pandering* is always evident. During performance the actors virtually construct the set of the play, redistribute space (expanding, contracting, deepening it) by means of props, sliding frames and drapes. The actors themselves are sometimes "constructed." Fitted at times with objects and cloth, they appear like assemblage art. In one scene dolls are strapped to the legs of the actresses for a musical number.

In the world of *Pandering*, where gesture is dissociated from language or merges with it, where language is fragmented and thought dislocated, time is experienced in terms of changing spatial relationships. In the design of the set Foreman plays purposefully with perspective: A road leading to a house at the back of the playing area narrows to its end ("Try looking through the wrong end of the telescope. Everything looks sharper, doesn't it?" asks the inquisitive VOICE). Many scenes are presented in slow motion, suggesting a two-dimensional, painterly perspective. The actors frequently stare at the audience or gaze sideways; other scenes are presented from the perspective of the picture-frame stage. The continual rearticulation of space which Foreman's long and deep but narrow loft theatre affords, complicates perception of movement and disorients the audience which must accordingly change its field of vision to accomodate the variety of spatial configurations.

Foreman's idiosyncratic use of strings, which dangle from the ceiling and stretch in horizontal rows or diagonal crosses about the performing space, sectionalizes space and cuts it into geometric shapes. Another use of the strings has more to do with Foreman's insistent directorial focus on elements within the stage picture: his pointing out certain correspondences between the words and the images. When a performer, for example, draws a string from one end of the space to another until it touches a person or object, that person or object is defined in an exact point of time and space, as well as in reference to other activities on stage. In this way the world of *Pandering* presents a diagrammatic reality whose system of reference is entirely within the play as performed. Foreman's work is conceptual art, i.e., self-defining.

The rhythmic element of the piece is carried from unit to unit. The sound of a metronome during the production articulates its beats, affirming the musicality of the work. Foreman's work in the theatre parallels the trance or minimal music of such diverse composers as Philip Glass, LaMonte Young, Terry Riley and Steve Reich in whose compositions the accretion of sound is a key structural feature. Glass, in particular, has written:

> . . . nothing happens in the usual sense . . .
> instead, the gradual accretion of musical material
> can and does serve as the basis of the listener's
> attention . . . neither memory nor anticipation . . .
> have a place in sustaining the texture, quality or
> reality of the musical experience.[2]

His statement accurately describes the ambience of *Pandering*, which is constructed from the gradual build-up of small units of composition.

Conversely, subtraction—pause or silence—is important to *Pandering* as an interruptive device and a way of slowing down the performance, as is playing the taped VOICE against the natural voices of the actors by subtracting them from their words. John Cage was the first to regard silence as a viable structural unit of music, overthrowing much of traditional compositional theory which had viewed time in music as an empty unit to be filled. In the dance world Yvonne Rainer and others of the Judson Dance Theater and post-Judson period experimented with time as duration and the subtraction of movement. They were often joined by artists such as Robert Rauschenberg and Robert Morris who worked very specifically with new concepts of movement through time and the placement of objects in space. Foreman has solid foundations in post-Cagean aesthetics as they have filtered through the worlds of art, music and dance. His exploration of movement and spatial organization, elasticization of time, and radical situation of ob-

[2]Program Note to a concert at Town Hall on May 6, 1973, at which Philip Glass and his ensemble performed "Another Look at Harmony, Parts 1 and 2."

jects in the construction of his productions have been, and still are, dominant preoccupations of New York avant-garde artists.

Foreman's application of silence is significantly demonstrated in his use of tableau—the subtraction of the moving image. Tableau is *Pandering's* chief unit of composition, a still life which frames the action and "quotes" it. This quoting of gesture is another Brechtian technique that finds expression in Foreman's theatre; however, Foreman's employment of tableau, because it occurs more frequently and lasts longer than Brechtian tableau, elasticizes time as well as continually disrupting the spatial flow of the production. In tableau Foreman's actors appear as frozen voids in space—like the chalk-white faceless forms in a Chirico landscape—until they are revived by the tape machine or a change of scenery.

Tableau is used in various ways: the duplication of gestures in foreground and background; close-up perspective; the inclusion of a single kinetic element in an otherwise frozen picture; a confrontation of the audience vis-à-vis the actors in a frontal position; and for iconographic effect. Finally, by employing tableaux which throw certain elements of the production into high relief, Foreman is able to bracket perception of events on stage, thereby drawing attention to particular elements of the stage picture.

The framing of events on stage is paralleled by the framing of objects in which a single element is presented in close-up against a larger, more complicated background of activity. For instance, in the palm of his hand an actor in a foreground position holds a letter in an envelope which is affixed to a plate: It is another way in which Foreman breaks the continuity of composition by extreme reduction of a scene or gesture. Windows, boxes and cutouts in the design of the set frame objects or people, such as RHODA'S breasts exhibited in a door frame.

Curiously, Foreman's published notes and manifestoes reiterate his fascination with framing. Sentences are often subdivided by parentheses, brackets and equation symbols; rather than flowing smoothly they focus on single elements.

The framing devices and the tableaux of *Pandering,* in addition to disrupting the flow of time, draw attention to its passage. Time exists, as it were, in the continuous present of the dream world where images of the subconscious appear, drift away and then reappear, or collide with other images. Space repeatedly changes its contours in defiance of physical laws so that a wall of a room gives way to a jungle and scenes shift easily from outdoors to indoors. The people who inhabit this surreal world are free to roam with abandon through a series of adventures that take them back and forth in time and place. It is the landscape of Foreman's mind, the image-activated visions of his subconscious. Scattered about in this world are fruit, an oversized horse and giant pencils, croquet balls, stuffed animals, a pistol, snake and bicycle—all of which have symbolic value in Foreman's psychodrama. These are the symbols of childhood, of violence, of power and fear, temptation and sensuality.

In his situation of objects and people in *Pandering* Foreman recalls similar styles of the personal, surrealist films of Jean Cocteau and the American experimentalist Maya Deren. Foreman shares with them his love of melodrama, eroticism of violence, the placement of the human figure against a plane, narcissism, and the distortion of time and space through the use of mirrors and walls. However, Foreman's work differs from their classical surrealism in its demand for rigorous control rather than spontaneous expression, the importance given to phenomenological activity, and its high degree of cerebralism. Seen in another light, Foreman's filmic inheritance may be what P. Adams Sitney observed as the American avant-garde cinema's unacknowledged aspiration: "The cinematic reproduction of the human mind."[3] *Pandering to the Masses: A Misrepresentation* is a *theatrical* reproduction of the human mind—Richard Foreman's. He creates in his theatre a new way of thinking about the theatre event, a greater consciousness of art. Not only does he make theatre going more meaningful, but life as well.

BONNIE MARRANCA

---

[3]P. Adams Sitney, *Visionary Film: The American Avant-Garde* (N.Y.: Oxford University Press, 1974), p. 408.

PREFACE :

RICHARD FOREMAN

The Ontological-Hysteric Theater (R. Foreman) originally presented *Pandering to the Masses: A Misrepresentation* from January through March 1975 at their theater in New York. It might be of interest for readers to bear in mind certain features of that production which I wrote, directed and designed.

The VOICE was always my taped voice. The majority of the remaining lines were also on tape. The four principal performers (RHODA, BEN, MAX, ELEANOR) recorded those, each separate word being spoken by a different one of those four performers in sequence, no matter who was listed in the script as the "speaker" of any particular line. The voice of each performer was isolated on one of four loudspeakers—one at each of the four corners of the audience. So, words bombarded the audience—a different voice for each word, each word coming from a different place. Superimposed on this, the performers on stage hearing their own lines (as RHODA, MAX, etc.) coming over the tape would then, softly, repeat a few key words of their speech in counterpoint to the ongoing tape.

The VOICE lines spoken by me were not so divided but delivered simply in a deep, measured voice coming from the furthest rear speaker.

In every scene, certain key lines were *not* on tape, and simply spoken live, for emphasis, by an actor.

In addition, it might be valuable to note that the play evolved over its two months of rehearsal in such a way that certain features grew out of the rather unusual performance space of the

12

Ontological-Hysteric Theater's loft. Consisting of a narrow room, the stage and audience area are both only 14 feet wide. While seven rows of audience seating measure about 16 feet in depth, the stage itself is a full 75 feet deep. The first 20 feet of that is at floor level, but the entire stage width from then on is built at a steep rake running the next 30 feet of depth, finally leveling off at about a six foot height for the remaining depth. During the performance people and objects would often roll down that 30 foot rake, and sliding walls would enter from the side of the stage, creating a series of quickly changing spaces which varied from 12 to the full 75 feet in depth.

RICHARD FOREMAN

THE ONTOLOGICAL-HYSTERIC THEATER (R. Foreman) premiered *Pandering To The Masses: A Misrepresentation* at the theatre's loft in New York on January 9, 1975. Richard Foreman wrote, directed and designed the work.

Max	Bob Fleischner
Leo	Stuart Sherman
Rhoda	Kate Manheim
Ben	John Erdman
Black Magician	Charles Bergengren
Eleanor	Aline Lillie Mayer
Sophia	Sheila McLaughlin

AND

Camille Foss, Ellen Mills LeCompte, Gregory Gubitosa, Richard Levine, Gail Conrad, Suzanne Oshry, Susan Siegel, John Matturri.

The text of *Pandering To The Masses: A Misrepresentation* does not indicate the division of speech between tape and actor.

PANDERING TO THE MASSES:
A MISREPRESENTATION

(The audience assembles. After a while, MAX enters up center, sits, and stares at the audience. Then a MAN enters and sits at a bicycle down center, fixed so that he can peddle rapidly; but the bicycle will not move. Then the lights on stage begin to brighten.)

VOICE: Ladies and gentlemen. This play, at its center, tells of Rhoda, who is still off stage, and her introduction into a secret society, which dispenses a very particular kind of knowledge, which Rhoda learns to endure, which Max, who sits up center, learns to think about. This knowledge has to do with energy, effort, difficulty, awkwardness, failure, and then, effort renewed.

(Music. MAN on bicycle begins to peddle furiously. After a while, the music fades.)

MAX: You . . . understand . . . *NOTHING*!

VOICE: Max . . . regretfully concludes, that you who watch and wait have unfortunately proven, through your actions and reactions, that certain subtle, exact, specific and necessary areas of understanding are not available to your—

(Sentence interrupted by a buzzer, followed by loud music. The music ends with a heavy thud.)

VOICE: Recapitulation—

(RHODA enters, discovers a letter in a downstage cabinet.)

—You understand nothing. Are you thinking at this moment. Do you think using the associative method. Everybody does, you know. Each thought is accompanied by overtones which are images which may not be pictures but are, certainly.

> (Buzzer. Music overlaps. RHODA, SOPHIA and ELEANOR revealed naked at the top of a hill. Three men run down the hill with giant pencils and wave them threateningly at MAX. Then the women start down the hill, and when the music stops, turn sideways in provocative poses. MAX is staring at them through a telescope.)

VOICE: Try looking through the wrong end of the telescope. Everything looks sharper, doesn't it.

> (Buzzer, with music, and MAX starts doing a shuffle dance at the telescope, as a wall of the room slides in and blocks his view of the women. Music fades but he continues his shuffle dance in silence.)

VOICE: The old theater would prove to you that Max is dancing the way that he is dancing, by which is meant his motives, proven real and genuine, and you are convinced in a way appropriate to the theater. The new theater doesn't convince you of anything like that but he keeps doing it, anyway.

> (MAX still dancing, then stops.)

VOICE: (Accompanied by soft thuds.) What you are watching at the present moment is the prologue to the play entitled *Pandering to the Masses: A Misrepresentation,* in which a certain intellectual context is made visible to the audience for that work. The play itself, *Pandering to the Masses: A Misrepresentation,* will begin in perhaps, five minutes.

MAX: (Holding out his hand.) Now, I want some water.

VOICE: Now, he reaches out his hand. What could go into his hand.

MAX: Another hand.

> (RHODA enters, puts her hand in his.)

RHODA: Oh Max. In your head, everything proceeds by association.

VOICE: Recapitulation: do you think using the associative method.

Everybody does. Each though is accompanied by overtones, which are images that may not be pictures but are, certainly.

MAX: (As a bell rings once.) I make something with my hands. Then I look at it and I say to myself, make it a second time. Then I really make it, plus, I do it without touching it.

(Music begins.)

VOICE: (Over music.) Additional material contained in the pro- logue to the play entitled *Pandering to the Masses: A Misrepresen- tation.*

(RHODA slowly reaches for her now naked breasts, and starts to knead them slowly, then faster and faster. The music stops and she freezes.)

MAX: I don't need an answer. I don't need a yes, yes, yes, yes.

VOICE: Recapitulation. I make something with my hands plus, I don't need an answer. I don't need a yes, yes, yes, yes.

MAX: I shouldn't be wasting my own time talking about it.

(A single note is struck.)

What a beautiful note. I think I'll take credit for it.

(Wall opens to reveal a lit lamp.)

Go back where you came from, lamp.

(Wall closes, MAX reaches into his pocket and brings out a tiny tree.)

Oh, oh, what's this. Humm, come closer everybody.

(Looking at the audience.)

On second thought, that's impossible.

(RHODA begins to cross the stage rear, in a wedding dress, as wall of room goes off and behind is a house, tiny, far away in the forest. A road with trees leads up to it.)

MAX: I'm looking for myself. I won't find it in a mirror.

RHODA: Look . . . at . . . me.

MAX: When she said the word "look," I thought of eyesight, by which I mean headlights.

(Pause.)

The next logical thing was a road, and the trees along the road, and oh . . .

VOICE: The associative experiment in the art of our era.

RHODA: It's not productive, is it.

> (Buzzer. Music overlaps and continues as the wall of the room returns, and MAX enters a little 'writing cabinet' and scratches away with his pencil on paper.)

MAX: I am now in the present moment. Writing it, of course, not when you are watching it.

> (He looks up.)

What can I do about that evident problem. Nothing. Nothing. I can proceed as if everything will take care of itself, and it will.

VOICE: You can either watch Max writing it, or you can watch what he is writing. But you can only watch what he is writing after he is writing it, and in that case your expectations are in a different direction, are they not.

MAX: It will be in the present, after it is in the present.

> (Buzzer, loud music.)

VOICE: The demon energy makes his second appearance of the year.

DEMON: (RHODA in disguise.) I: Want: To: Eat: People.

VOICE: But of course. But of course he wants to eat people, because his appetite is insatiable. Like the great beast himself, eating is what he does best. He . . . sits down.

> (Buzzer, loud music. No one moves.)

VOICE: He . . . sits down.

> (RHODA sits on a naked woman, one of several who lie about, decorating the floor of MAX's writing chamber. Pause. Then music begins, and the scene shifts. MAX is now sitting on the chair in the center of a large, empty room. As the music continues, women strut across the stage rear, in a line, arms linked, little dolls strapped to their shins. They glare at MAX as they move sideways across the stage, in step to the music. Several times, MAX falls off his chair but recovers and re-seats himself. A voice is heard whispering as the music fades.)

VOICE: Oh Max, Max, Oh Max, Max, Max, Max, Max, Max, Max, Oh Max, Max, Max, Ohhh, Max, Max, Oh Max, Oh Max, Oh Max, do you want, Max, do you want, Max, do you want to be rewarded because you are such a good writer? Oh Max, Max, Max, do you want us to give you a reward?

(MAX smiles and nods his head. Silence.)

Ladies and gentleman, announcing the ending of the prologue and the beginning of the play proper, entitled *Pandering to the Masses: A Misrepresentation.*

(Pause.)

He. Sits down.

(Pause.)

He. Sits down.

(The wall of MAX's study returns. Now RHODA is in the room.)

He. Sits down.

MAX: Nothing has to happen.

VOICE: Clarification. Clarification. Max, famous writer of more than a dozen works, immortal amongst his friends and acquaintances, seeks now, a new perspective, and so invites in his imagination, a replacement figure, to mediate between himself and his beloved Rhoda.

(MAX is now on his hands and knees, trying to write on a pad that is held on the floor in front of him and slowly pulled out of the room, making him follow. BEN has entered behind him and now sits in his chair.)

Leaving the room on all fours, his chair filled by the younger and more ambitious Ben, he composes . . . even as he is exiting. Knowing he will return, eventually, and Rhoda, transformed perhaps, will be awaiting him.

BEN: It's only music.

RHODA: What music.

BEN: Oh Rhoda, I don't think we can hear music coming over our own—

VOICE: RA . . . DI . . . O.

BEN: Oh Rhoda, it's only light.

VOICE: Light.

RHODA: Did you say it's only music. Did you say it's only light.

> (Wall of room disappears to reveal a jungle behind. Naked SOPHIA and ELEANOR are there, walking slowly off.)

Did you say it's only decoration. Oh Ben, I don't know what it means when it means it.

BEN: Here. Would you take my hand.

RHODA: Bandage it, huh.

BEN: No Rhoda, it's already bandaged.

> (Music begins, and MAX enters with a large bandage on his right hand, wearing a pith helmet.)

VOICE: His *WRITING* hand.

> (MAX sits in the jungle, holding out his hand for inspection as the music fades.)

MAX: Look. I bandaged my hand myself.

> (Pause.)

You think I can't write. It was a decision that was not my decision.

VOICE: Recapitulation. He bandaged it himself.

> (Music again as people enter and now bandage BEN's hand.)

His writing hand.

> (Music fades. RHODA finds a glove in a cabinet and puts it on.)

RHODA: I prefer wearing a glove to wearing a bandage.

BEN: —Text, text, that's what counts. Not music, not ideas, not light, not decor, not—

> (Buzzer. Jungle drop opens to reveal a second jungle behind it. SOPHIA and ELEANOR there, naked, striding downstage in step to the music which has begun.)

SOPHIA and ELEANOR: Which one of us is Sophia (Eleanor).

RHODA: I know one thing. It's not me.

BEN and MAX: (Point.) Rhoda! Rhoda! Rhoda!

BEN: —Prove it.

(RHODA crosses and puts on a second glove.)

SOPHIA and ELEANOR: He's putting everything he knows into this play.

BEN: Everything?

VOICE: He always puts everything he knows, into every play he writes. In this play for instance, you will see that the naked Sophia and the naked Eleanor are in possession of a certain kind of knowledge to which Rhoda, not yet certain that she needs or desires it, will be soon, painfully, initiated.

RHODA: Everything is easy to come by. For instance, did you know that as I reached for my gloves inside the drawer—

VOICE: You didn't exactly reach for them, Rhoda.

RHODA: —I noticed a letter, addressed to me, lying inside the cabinet.

> (Music. A ruffle of feathers placed around SOPHIA's neck, leaves around ELEANOR's neck.)

SOPHIA: Which do you like better, feathers or leaves.

RHODA: A letter. A letter.

BEN and MAX: Don't forget to find out what it is in the letter.

> (Music begins as MAX's writing cabinet is wheeled in, and opened to reveal a black-faced MAGICIAN sitting inside, a letter pressed to his forehead.)

MAGICIAN and RHODA: Letter letter on the brow
Who is chastened, pure—allow
That being, black or white
To penetrate the deep delight
Of Rhoda's mystery wisdom where
The brain falls down in miles of hair
The hair like clouds upon the sun
Which hide the truth from everyone.

MAGICIAN: I. See. A. Word.

VOICE: What word!

> (Music, blackout. Scene shifts to outdoors, the little house on the hill in the distance. BEN sits curled up on the side of the hill.)

BEN: What word do you think the—

VOICE: —There *ARE* no *BLACK MAGICIANS.*

BEN: He pressed the letter to his forehead and then he saw a word.

> (RHODA enters, stops.)

RHODA: That looks like—

BEN: Oh? Do you still have those gloves on.

RHODA: You shouldn't be thinking about my gloves, Ben.

> (Pause. ELEANOR enters.)

By the way.

ELEANOR: Hello, Rhoda and Ben.

RHODA: (Turns.) My rival.

> (Pause. ELEANOR crosses and slaps RHODA with a glove. Then they hold each other tightly, as if in a frozen struggle.)

What perfume are you wearing.

ELEANOR: That's not perfume, that's my own body odors. I can smell yours too.

RHODA: But I'm wearing perfume.

> (Enter MAX wearing a long nose.)

MAX: Ladies, you'll never guess what I just smelled.

ALL: Shhhhhh.

BEN: This looks like my room.

> (Pause.)

What I think is, what kind of a person lives in such a room.

> (Pause. He pulls his coat around his shoulders.)

It's getting cool, isn't it.

> (Blackout, scene shifts to indoors, as RHODA goes to the cabinet and finds a letter.)

VOICE: Rhoda does not know, still, what is expected of her. Rivals? In knowledge? If she is alone against the stripped wall of her own living room, are her experiences and her anticipations any the less full of imaginary fears? Body experiences? The stripes have something to do with her body. The letter, she finds, has something to do with her nervousness.

RHODA: You know what's in this letter.

BEN: No.

RHODA: It invites me to join a certain society.

BEN: What society.

> (Pause.)

RHODA: A certain society concerned with knowledge.

BEN: I'm not interested.

RHODA: In knowledge?

BEN: It's a dead end.

RHODA: Don't be so sure.

VOICE: Knowledge she decides, is a dead end.

> (Soft music begins, RHODA takes the letter and moves it over her body, ending up on the floor.)

RHODA: Eleanor and Sophia are already members of this society.

> (All are on stage now, watching her.)

RHODA: No men, just women—

VOICE: She doesn't know how to say it, but. . .

RHODA: It involves hurting each other and making discoveries.

BEN: That's a dead end Rhoda.

VOICE: Knowledge she decides, is a dead end.

RHODA: I don't think so. I don't think so.

> (Wall of the room gives way to the jungle. SOPHIA and ELEANOR there, naked, as RHODA sprawls in an uncomfortable position on the floor to look at them.)

SOPHIA and ELEANOR: Step over here into the jungle, Rhoda.

VOICE: She resorts to bad posture, because it would be more comfortable to believe, like Ben, that knowledge was a dead end. But she knows he doesn't really believe that.

RHODA: If I'm going to get undressed, I think it should be in private.

(She undresses behind a screen, then reappears and points at BEN.)

RHODA: How about you.

BEN: I thought I couldn't be a member of this knowledge society.

(Pause, then BEN undresses.)

O.K. I'm ready for knowledge too.

(Pause. A thud, and PEOPLE enter to hold books and leaves under everyone's noses. All sniff.)

VOICE: They are all, drenched with meaning.

RHODA: Oh, look at this leaf.

ELEANOR: Tell you what.

ALL: Ahhhhhh!

VOICE: The "Ahhhh!" of recognition, announces the beginning of the play *Fear,* which happens to Rhoda in the center of the play entitled *Pandering to the Masses: A Misrepresentation.*

(Set changes, the front curtain of a stage. BEN stands covering his eyes, soft piano music, as a disguised MAX peeks through the curtains.)

Fear enters, left of center. He goes and touches Ben's forehead for reasons that are clear, though not visible.

BEN: Fear . . . has no effect upon me. He remains invisible, which is one reason for his lack of effect, but there are other reasons.

RHODA: (Appears through the curtain.) Oh, Ben.

BEN: What.

(Pause.)

What.

RHODA: (Covering her eyes.) 1   2   3   4   5

VOICE: The play *Fear* continues, by demonstrating what it is that apparently frightens the invisible Ben, which means the doubly invisible Max, which means that what is frightening is invisible now to the mathematical power 3, 4, 5, 6, 7, 8, 9.

(VOICE gets softer and fades out as the soft music continues and the curtain opens to reveal RHODA sitting on a large rock which is slowly descending the hill with the small house in the distance. The rock reaches the bottom of the hill, RHODA rises and goes to a small table on which a bottle sits. She lifts the bottle to reveal an egg underneath. She picks up the egg and slowly crosses the stage, now followed step by step by the BLACK MAGICIAN. She stops, frightened.)

RHODA: Oh. It would hurt less if I put my forehead against the little egg.

(She does so.)

Wrong on two counts. Nothing hurt, and what happened took my breath away.

(She looks at the audience as a disguised MAX appears on the other side of the stage and slowly reaches for a second egg, lying on the floor.)

Didn't it take your breath away too. I know it took my breath away someplace.

(MAX holds his egg in the air now, between two fingers. RHODA imitates his pose.)

RHODA: Oh, I understand perfectly. That egg is part of a diagram.

(Pause.)

That egg is part of a diagram, and a picnic, it is not.

(She hooks her egg onto a string from above. A loud noise, and the wall of a room comes in. A legend is projected on a screen:

"Fear enters
and speaks to Rhoda
with his soft voice.
Fear proposes
a network
and a joint accomplishment."

An elderly couple occupy the room.)

OLD MAN: Fear knows his task well, wouldn't you say.

OLD WOMAN: Quite well.

OLD MAN: We both agree. Fear knows his task quite well. Rhoda knows her task, also.

RHODA: Suddenly I'm not frightened.

> (She thinks.)

Fear left quick, didn't he.

> (She turns to her egg on its string, and makes it swing back and forth.)

That's all there is to that.

> (She turns to go, at which point BEN rises from the floor where he has been sleeping.)

BEN: Rhoda. I want to thank you for solving my biggest problem for me, Rhoda.

> (Pause. RHODA turns back in the doorway, watching him.)

My biggest problem was fear, and you solved it.

RHODA: I did, did I.

BEN: You solved it, Rhoda.

RHODA: Sleep.

BEN: I wouldn't say sleep solved my problems, but it solved my problems. What was inside of me got outside fast, and that solved my problems.

> (PEOPLE run on stage and hold leaves under everyone's noses.)

BEN: We imagine it, and then we sleep, and solve it.

ALL: Ahhhh!

VOICE: The "Ahhh!" of recognition announces the return to the central narrative of the play entitled *Pandering to the Masses: A Misrepresentation.*

> (Wall opens to a larger room. At the rear are RHODA, SOPHIA and ELEANOR, all wearing large false noses.)

—in which Sophia, Eleanor, and the not yet fully initiated Rhoda, turn their attention back to subjects not yet fully resolved, such as leaf: fragrance: nose: knowing: thinking.

ELEANOR: Put the leaf under my nose.

BEN: I see. I see.

> (Leaves held under their noses.)

RHODA, SOPHIA, ELEANOR: Ahhhhhhh!

BEN: Nobody has yet thought that knowledge could enter through the nose.

> (Pause.)

You understand. People have said—

VOICE: Thought.

> (PEOPLE press books to the faces of RHODA, SOPHIA and ELEANOR who then collapse.)

BEN: —knowledge could come through the ear, through the eye, even through the mouth, i.e. the mouth speaks and discovers things in so doing. But nobody has said, "Ah yes, through the nose."

RHODA: (From the floor.) Didn't you remember.

BEN: (Turns to look at her.) What.

> (Letters placed between the knees of the three women on the floor.)

RHODA: Didn't it occur to you that maybe I was

BEN: What.

> (Soft music starts.)

RHODA: Smelling. The letter.

VOICE: That's impossible. It wasn't Rhoda. It was the Black Magician. Plus, it was at his forehead, not under his nose.

> (BEN goes and rests his elbows on the table, looking straight into a mirror.)

VOICE: That said, he looks into the glass and smells . . . nothing.

> (Wall of the smaller room returns.)

BEN: The stripped wall.

VOICE: What is it.

BEN: The beginning.

VOICE: The beginning of what.

> (Pause.)

BEN: That too has something to do with my thought process.

VOICE: What.

BEN: The jungle was a peripheral consideration.

VOICE: How can you be so sure.

> (Loud drum music, as a legend is projected on a screen:
>> "He goes to the wall
>> finds two peep-holes
>> (one for each eye)
>> and looks through to where Rhoda,
>> Sophia and Eleanor were naked,
>> and were dancing."
>
> A panel in the wall opens, and the women take turns showing their naked breasts. The music changes as a man comes to the downstage bicycle and again peddles furiously, and BEN and MAX roll about clutching large stuffed animals. RHODA, SOPHIA and ELEANOR strut insolently back and forth across the stage. Then the music ends and all freeze.)

ALL: What next. What next.

MAX: More music.

VOICE: Pretty frustrated for a person, huh.

> (Pause.)

MAX: What about this secret society.

VOICE: Ohhhhhhhhhhhh

> (RHODA, SOPHIA and ELEANOR start fighting amongst themselves as the scene shifts to a banquet table. All the others now grouped about the table, waiting. Then ELEANOR slaps RHODA. A silence. Then RHODA picks up a piece of cake and pushes it into ELEANOR's face.)

ELEANOR: Why did you do that, Rhoda.

> (MAN downstage on bicycle is offered some cake, which he starts eating slowly with his fingers, as MAX appears in the far rear and seats himself on a kind of throne.)

RHODA: I wanted to see if she'd "fight back."

ELEANOR: I can't fight back with cake all over my face.

BEN: (At the table.) I think I'm cured.

MAX: Not yet. You still have to have more adventures.

BEN: Does it take adventures to be cured.

> (Pause. Then RHODA picks up another piece of cake, and pushes it very deliberately into her own face.)

BEN: That's very interesting. You put cake on your face also.

> (Someone at the table opens a fan and starts fanning BEN, as RHODA grabs for ELEANOR and, faces still covered with cake, they fight for a moment and then freeze.)

RHODA: Would you hold that fan between our faces please.

BEN: Why.

RHODA: (Pause.) We don't like each other.

BEN: It seems to me you're better friends than you admit.

ELEANOR: Friends!

RHODA: —This is how much I like the little shit.

> (Again a moment of violent struggle, then they freeze, and RHODA shouts to BEN.)

Hold! It! There!

BEN: Where.

RHODA: Hold! It! There!

> (He holds it between their faces.)

What do you think.

BEN: I'm not.

RHODA and ELEANOR: Liar! Liar!

> (Another violent flurry, then freeze.)

RHODA: Hold! It! There!

> (He does so, and ELEANOR starts to sob.)

What do you think now.

BEN: Stop hurting her.

RHODA: She's hurting me too, you know. Why don't *YOU* take over for me.

BEN: Doing what.

RHODA: I bet you could beat her up easily, Ben.

MAX: Have some cake first.

BEN: I couldn't eat.

> (Someone enters, carrying a piece of cake to BEN, and pushes it into his face. Then another flurry of fighting between ELEANOR and RHODA, then ELEANOR leaves RHODA and attacks BEN. He subdues her, he relaxes, and she attacks again. Legend on the screen:
>> "The minute he relaxes
>> she attacks him again."

BEN: (Held to the floor by ELEANOR, as he holds her head under his arm.) Stop that!

> (RHODA takes the fan and holds it between BEN and ELEANOR's face.)

RHODA: Oh Ben, can't you move now.

BEN: Look, look, what I'm holding under my arm.

ALL: Be calm, Ben.

BEN: I can't be calm when I have to.

ELEANOR: You're hurting me.

BEN: I tried to be calm, but I couldn't be calm.

RHODA: Stupid.

ALL: —STUPID!

RHODA: —who do you want to change places with.

BEN: Nobody.

RHODA: Here I am.

BEN: Nobody.

> (Music starts, scene shifts, with three rocking chairs placed at the top of the hill.)

VOICE: Knowledge, she decides, is a dead end. Still, she amazingly affirms her dedication to its necessity, its frustrations, and its violent self-divisions.

> (RHODA, SOPHIA, ELEANOR now seated rocking in the rocking chairs.)

SOPHIA: This is just one more of the many ways to knowledge.

ELEANOR: I hope she didn't get hurt.

RHODA: Who.

ALL: Rhoda.

RHODA: When.

ALL: During the fighting.

RHODA: It didn't last long enough.

> (They rock for a while, then stop.)

SOPHIA: What were your sensations.

> (Jungle drop covers the scene, MAGICIAN there with a big cigar.)

VOICE: What he likes to do is have white girls entertain him in his—

ALL: What.

VOICE: Tent.

> (BEN enters, frowns.)

BEN: That's *my* tent.

> (A tent is set up quickly.)

VOICE: Believe it or not, they have the same tent, and what is more, the same entertainment.

RHODA: We entertain each other, not pricks like you two.

BEN: Didn't you mean to say—

RHODA: What.

> (BEN points to the MAGICIAN, as two assistants come and hold letters to the MAGICIAN's brow.)

BEN: He can do one of two things. Read your mind or read through a sealed envelope.

MAGICIAN: Wait.

ALL: What.

MAGICIAN: Am I really as black as I seem.

> (He takes off his black mask, BEN steps toward him.)

BEN: My brother.

MAGICIAN: You didn't recognize me.

BEN: I didn't want to recognize you.

> (They embrace as the tent opens and MAX is revealed sitting inside, nervously wiping his brow.)

MAX: There is a very dangerous thing that could happen to me here. All energy.

ALL: What.

MAX: Where does it come from.

> (Music. A horse enters. Music fades as the MAGICIAN goes to the horse.)

VOICE: Then he says— Can I give you a lift.

MAGICIAN: Don't be frightened.

BEN: I'd forgotten you existed.

RHODA: I don't like to say this, but—

BEN: What.

SOPHIA: She finds your brother more attractive than you, Ben.

BEN: So what.

VOICE: Maybe it's only because she has an after image of the disguise he was wearing.

RHODA: I'd like to see you both on the same horse.

> (Soft music. BEN slowly climbs onto the horse behind the MAGICIAN.)

BEN: O.K.

MAGICIAN: We never liked each other, did we.

BEN: We never even liked the same entertainment.

VOICE: Then he says— Don't fall off.

> (Loud noise and thuds as a big snake is wound around BEN, MAGICIAN and horse.)

RHODA: I think the horse has had it.

SOPHIA: Do you mean it got bit, by a snake.

RHODA: More like a python, which doesn't bite, but squeezes.

> (ELEANOR enters, holding up a small snake.)

ELEANOR: It wasn't a python. It was more famous and more useful.

> (RHODA crosses and twists SOPHIA's leg as tent and horse vanish and all the women are crying.)

VOICE: You see, as she said, every experience, though perhaps peripheral to primary revelation of knowledge, friendship and inventiveness, still every experience can be a learning experience, if allowed to take its place in the mapping process of one's private adventure and spatial self-orientation.

RHODA: What about the decor.

SOPHIA: It was painted.

ELEANOR: Is *THIS* painted or do you mean oh— that isn't decor.

> (Loud music. All enter. MAN who goes to bicycle stops just before climbing on, aims a gun and fires at audience.)

VOICE: (Over music.) Fire once, toward the offending serpent. Cover one's eyes and shoot, like a blind man.

> (MAN is now on bicycle, peddling furiously as others dance maniacally in the background. The music fades, but they dance on in the silence, as ELEANOR re-enters holding up her snake.)

ELEANOR: Unfortunately sir, you killed—

VOICE: Why does she say unfortunately.

ELEANOR: —my snake.

VOICE: What's unfortunate about it.

ELEANOR: Well. . .

VOICE: It means *YOU'LL* have to be punished.

RHODA: How.

VOICE: (As RHODA pantomimes being beaten.) Punishment, says Rhoda, isn't the worst turn of events. Because Ben learns what he knows through books, which have chapters. But I learn what I know from having adventures, and I don't know how to put that into a book.

> (Buzzer and music, as SOPHIA runs on with a giant snake and fights with RHODA, trying to wrap her in it. The music fades and the struggle subsides.)

SOPHIA: Doesn't hurt much, does it.

RHODA: Do I get to try it on your—

(SOPHIA steps back from her, hands on hips.)

SOPHIA: Try it.

RHODA: What.

SOPHIA: Try it.

RHODA: I'm all tied up.

SOPHIA: Can't you imagine you're getting squeezed.

RHODA: That's what I'd like to try on you.

SOPHIA: You don't get the point.

RHODA: What.

ELEANOR: (Entering.) Somebody's shot my snake!

(Thud. RHODA screams as the big snake squeezes her and she thrashes about. Wall of the room returns, and a giant horse comes in the room, and BEN and MAGICIAN immediately enter and climb on it. SOPHIA enters and the music fades.)

BEN and MAGICIAN: We heard that somebody needed help.

(Door opens, and there is RHODA, wrapped in the giant snake.)

RHODA: Untie me.

BEN and MAGICIAN: Can we be of assistance.

(A bell rings, they dismount and untie her.)

VOICE: They untie Rhoda. Then, she tries to come to certain conclusions.

(RHODA, freed, takes the snake and tries to wrap it around SOPHIA who fights her off.)

ELEANOR: Somebody shot my snake.

VOICE: *YOU* can do it better.

ALL: What.

(RHODA and SOPHIA still struggling.)

VOICE: *YOU* can do *ANYTHING* better.

(SOPHIA pins RHODA to the wall. A firing squad hurries on and fires once. All is suddenly quiet.)

VOICE: Bullets are, to her, like messages.

> (Pause. SOPHIA exists and RHODA leans against the wall.)

VOICE: Thinking for herself, at last.

> (RHODA is blindfolded as very loud, ominous music begins. A letter held up rear, and RHODA stumbles toward it, seizes it, then as if in a trance crosses rear holding up the letter as if she were a target in a shooting gallery.
>
> (The VOICE speaks over the loud music as the guns fire again and again.)

VOICE: She, has to. . . !

> (More music and shots.)

VOICE: She, avoided everything.

> (Music slowly fades, and RHODA faces front, lowering letter and removing blindfold.)

VOICE: Dead space.

> (Pause. RHODA goes and touches the horse.)

VOICE: Dead space. Filled only by the return of Max, who left, but remained all the while, thinking about what was happening and wondering what he could say, to prove that everything was happening, the way it was supposed to be happening.

> (MAX appears in the door, wearing a crown. He raises a finger.)

MAX: Ah yes. You *know* what word is needed here.

VOICE: Ad-van-tageous. Ad-van-tageous.

> (Loud noise, VOICE loud over it, as MAX nods wisely.)

IKON! IKON! IKON!

> (Noise stops and VOICE continues as MAX and RHODA are framed with halos.)

VOICE: He inhabits that word. That means, to celebrate his return, finally, he thinks about his face as being her face. And thinks about his person as being her person, finally. And worships it, finally. And reads it, finally, like a wonderful book.

RHODA: You mean he—

ALL: Yes.

RHODA: Proof.

VOICE: That was the word *YOU* were thinking of.

RHODA: Was. . .

MAX: *I* was.

RHODA: (To audience.) That was the word *YOU* were thinking of. Here. Let's do the dance of the ikons.

> (Wall opens to reveal floral arches and a crowd of people all of whom fall to the floor, amidst open books which are scattered about. Then people start to crawl to the books, as MAX climbs on the big horse and is given a decorated lance and shield.)

VOICE: Now, finally, they are opening the door to the mind.

> (Everyone studying the books.)

Oh Max, you will be rewarded, if you can achieve certain things. Do you understand that if *HE* is rewarded, you are *ALL* rewarded.

> (Soft march music is heard in the distance, as the VOICE speaks quietly to the audience.)

The play is over. But the meaning of the play will be found within the pages of the books scattered across the floor. Such works including: *The Phenomenology of the Spirit* by Frederich Hegel; *The Cartesian Meditations* by Edmund Hauptfriel; *The Introduction to Logic and Aesthetics* by Morris Shlicksberg; and, of course, the text of *Pandering to the Masses: A Misrepresentation.*

> (Pause. Actors are looking at the audience.)

Ladies and gentlemen. The performers have been instructed to remain placed upon the stage where you now see them, until such time as the departure of spectators is well under way. We urge you, therefore, to begin leaving the theater. The performers will respect their instructions, and will not leave the stage until your focus has sufficiently shifted *FROM* that on-stage area. We *URGE* you, therefore, to begin leaving the theater.

> (March music continues softly, as chimes ring out in the distance, lights come up in the audience, and the play is over.)

A LETTER FOR QUEEN VICTORIA
ROBERT WILSON

ROBERT WILSON:
BYRD HOFFMAN
SCHOOL FOR BYRDS

Robert Wilson refers to *A Letter for Queen Victoria* as an opera; yet, lacking singers, its arias are merely verbal declamations. Nonetheless, the vision of this work is operatic, structured by themes that recur throughout the performance like leitmotifs, rather than by conventional plot. In its Wagnerian opulence *Queen Victoria* is a modern day *Gesamtkunstwerk,* unifying all the arts in a spiritual atmosphere of illusion and mysticism. It is an attempt by Wilson to lead his audience into what Wagner called "a spiritualized state of clairvoyance."

Architectonic in shape, *Queen Victoria* has four acts: four basic stage pictures framed by the same scene at beginning and end. A string quartet plays music throughout the entire performance, while the dance element is provided by two dancers who spin continuously on downstage ramp areas. Unlike most avant-garde theatre pieces, *Queen Victoria* is designed for a proscenium, with costumed performers and elaborate use of stage properties. It is a spectacle for our time descended from nineteenth-century Wagnerian opera.

Since it has no narrative structure, there is no real beginning or end to the piece. It exists rather in a continuous present. Each act begins with a tableau, gradually adding people to it; often objects appear (water tank, rock, lettuce, crocodile) when they seemingly have no function or relationship to events on stage. Performers, most of whom are numbered (up to four) rather than named, play more than one role in the production. The process of transformation is continuous.

39

In *Queen Victoria* incongruity is a stylistic feature; theatrical elements are autonomous, syncretist. It is not surprising, therefore, that Wilson's unification of diverse theatrical elements and situations should demonstrate his easy accommodation to the modernist heritage. From the Dadaist-Futurist-Surrealist past he has absorbed the belief in the value of simultaneous experience.

Similarly, *Queen Victoria* embraces numerous different themes and topics of discussion: human interaction, murder, the Civil War, justice, ecology, pilots and a plane crash, cultural imperialism, ancient civilizations and the atom bomb. Wilson emphasizes both communication between people and destruction of people. This leads one to believe that, on one level at least, *Queen Victoria* can be interpreted as a socio-political statement on human affairs. Yet Wilson's solution to the problem is not an ideological one; as his juxtaposition of images proves, it is a romantic, utopian one.

The pilots' scene in Act II, for example, with its frequent mention of a plane crash, coupled with the sounds of bombs exploding, suggests a vision of holocaust. That scene points to Wilson's apocalyptic vision, especially when viewed in the context of the preceding garden scene which indicates cosmic harmony, innocence and freedom from corruption. As a romantic, Wilson looks toward the purification of a cruel, unjust world and a return to an Edenic existence. *Queen Victoria* posits a new society.

Christopher Knowles, the autistic teenager in Wilson's company, represents pre-consciousness, innocence and futurity. When viewed in this context, the figure of Knowles increases in significance. In Jungian terms he is the "child archetype," the wonder-child, divine-child. Jung believed the mythological idea of the child was a symbol, not a copy, of an empirical child. Wilson, however, has gone beyond Jung because he uses Knowles not as symbol but as actuality.[1] Knowles is a natural wonder-child whose autism bestows on him extraordinary powers. When he flies across the stage (in a harness) in Act II he seems surely a *deus ex machina*.

If Wilson treats certain universal archetypes, he also deals with American cultural myths. A Civil War soldier apears intermittently throughout the performance, dialogue from gangster B-movies is recognizable, there are bombings and talk of foreign

---

[1]Carl Jung, "The Psychology of the Child Archetype," in *Psyche and Symbol,* ed. Violet S. de Laszlo (N.Y.: Doubleday Anchor, 1958), p. 124.

lands: All of these elements suggest Wilson's attitude toward American life. Finally, in a portion of the text which Knowles wrote, homage is paid to a Wild West hero, the Sundance Kid, in a long verbal aria that builds from the rhythm of a single line, "THE SUNDANCE KID IS BEAUTIFUL."

References to American culture come and go in *Queen Victoria,* which is composed of "ready-mades"—bits and pieces of overheard conversation, clichés, newspapers, television, radio and movies. This is theatre as assemblage art. Words are used merely for their sound and music value; language is completely "throwaway" and meaningless in content. Grounded in an aesthetic of dissonance, the production begins and ends with screams (aural tableaux that complement visual tableaux); scream songs, grunts and shrieks are frequent as are fabricated words like "SPUPS," "PIRUP," "HAP" and "HATH." Pure sound is important too, as gunshots, bomb blasts, horses' hooves and train whistles. The effect is that of a sound collage made from the juxtaposition of numerous textures and rhythms of sounds. Just as *Queen Victoria* is founded on movement minus time and character minus personality, sound has no meaning.

Wilson is an alchemist experimenting with words, freeing them from the constraint of syntactic logic. His results confirm what Hugo Ball claimed the Dadaists discovered: "The evangelical concept of the 'word' (logos) as a magical complex of images."[2] In *Queen Victoria* Wilson conjures up a new world where objects, movements, attitudes and gestures form the vocabulary of a visual language which replaces the verbal one. It is a world of narrative images which transcend materiality. Approaching Artaudian "metaphysics-in-action," it recovers some of the religious and mystical qualities that have been lost to modern theatre. Wilson takes characters, objects and situations having no common history nor relationship to each other, and merges them in a poetry of space that Artaud would have found humorous in its "anarchic dissociation."[3]

Disconnected from their usual meanings, words lack signifying structures, and instead, organize themselves into sound poetry. Yet, taken as a whole, thematic threads come together in

---

[2]Hugo Ball, "Dada Fragments (1916-1917)," in *The Dada Painters and Poets,* ed. Robert Motherwell (New York: Wittenborn, Schultz, 1951), p. 52.

[3]Antonin Artaud, "Metaphysics and the Mise-En-Scène," in *The Theatre and its Double,* trans. Mary Caroline Richards (New York: Grove Press, 1958), pp. 33-47.

the language of *Queen Victoria* because of repetition and the coupling of words with powerful sound and visual images. For example, in Act II pilots talk about faraway lands, their speech punctuated by the sounds of gunfire and bomb blasts, their figures silhouetted in angular shafts of light and dark. This scene alludes to American imperialism and destruction. There very definitely is "meaning" in this "meaningless" text. Act IV even offers a comment on the text, and by the Chinaman:

> A PERSON APPEARS IN A PLACE FOR A LENGTH OF TIME,
> INTERACTING WITH OTHERS, AND GOES—NOTHING UNUSUAL
> IN THAT . . . A PERSON APPEARS IN ANOTHER PLACE FOR THE
> EXACT SAME LENGTH OF TIME, INTERACTING IDENTICALLY
> WITH THE SAME NUMBER OF PEOPLE DOWN TO THE SMALLEST
> DETAILS—WHO CAN KNOW THAT ONE IS PART OF THE OTHER?
> . . . WHO CAN RECOGNIZE THE SAME NAMES, THE SAME
> FACES, THE SAME COURSE OF EVENTS? ONLY ONE WITH A
> VIEW OF SUFFICIENT BREADTH AND PATIENCE.

> (ACT IV, SECTION 1)

Queen Victoria is an exercise in the sharpness of sense perception. Wilson seems to ask: How many in the audience can remember speeches, situations and themes carried from one act to another? Since they have no conversational dialogue, the actors speak in sentences which, like echoes, are transmitted from one act to another. The same verbal exchange is repeated three times in Act I; parts of Act I emerge in Act II. Repetitive structures weave in and out of the various settings belying a sharp social criticism. The actual letter for Queen Victoria which introduces the production makes English look like a second language. In another age our contemporary English will probably sound as archaic. Wilson does not accept the absolutism of language and so he purposely sets out to fashion one to his own liking.

The text, written as a collaborative effect of the company (and shaped by Wilson), is filled with misspellings, incorrect grammar and punctuation, and syntactic errors in utter disregard for the significance of the *Word*. When two or more people speak to each other their discourse is completely irrational; words have no communicative value among personages in this drama. For instance:

> 1   MANDA SHE LOVE A GOOD JOKE YOU KNOW. SHE A LAWYER
>   TOO.
> 2   LET'S WASH SOME DISHES.
> 1   WHAT DO YOU DO MY DEAR?
> 2   OH, SHE'S A SOCIAL WORKER

Act I. Cynthia Lubar, Sheryl Sutton.   Photo © Johan Elbers.

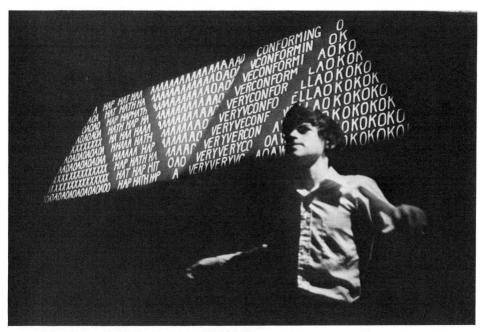

Entr'Acte #1. Christopher Knowles.   Photo © Johan Elbers.

Act III. Alma Hamilton.   Photo © Johan Elbers.

Act IV. Scotty Snyder, Stefan Brecht, Cynthia Lubar, Sheryl Sutton, George Ashley.   Photo © Johan Elbers.

1   NICE TRY GRACE
2   MANDA THERE ARE NO ACCIDENTS

(ACT I, SECTION 2)

There is a different style of speech—a new social gestus—in each of the acts of *Queen Victoria*. Perhaps the one which most resembles intelligible, albeit banal, speech—the sentences at least have a certain logic as bits of overheard conversation—is the Chitter-Chatter sequence of Act III. Here five couples, seated against a large backdrop painted in a symmetrical arrangement (like concrete poetry) of the words "chitter" and "chatter," gossip about trivial events until they fall over one by one at the sound of gunfire off-stage. As they speak they gesticulate wildly—five pairs of hands wave in the air like semaphores—so that the result is a merger of gesture and speech in semantic space. This Ionesco-esque scene clearly satirizes language as a serious mode of communication; as such, it is the most explicit section of the opera.

Queen Victoria is one long laugh at language's claim to supremacy in the realm of communicative possibilities. Instead of our highly industrialized society ruled by the phonetic alphabet, and thus by linear thought, *Queen Victoria* creates a prelinguistic world where sounds and gestures have richly symbolic and imagistic capabilities and the power to forge a new grammar of human interaction. It is a theatrical language, a visual semantics, which appeals to the senses, not to the intellect—an alphabet of signs.

Perhaps the best examples of Wilson's transformation of language are in the entr'actes he performs with Knowles (sometimes against a "break drop" of a dam overflowing with words). The entr'actes recapitulate past events or announce future events in the piece; they function as word or sound games—private language exercises. One of the significant features of the entr'actes is their incorporation of behavior patterns of autistic children in the theatrical performance: repetition, echolalia, wordplay, imitation. (Knowles is clinically diagnosed as autistic though Wilson firmly believes he simply has other perceptual powers than those considered "normal" in our society.) In the entr'actes the two build rhythms by shouting back and forth letters of the alphabet, and by clapping wooden blocks together; they play with certain clusters of letters ("HAP," "HATH," "HAT"), and put together words, letters and sentences like building blocks (combinations of "A," "O," "OK"). A sequence about "electro wheels" (autistic children are fascinated by circular shapes) builds to an exhilarating crescendo. Grounded in the dynamics of the personal relationship that Wilson and

Knowles share, these "musical" duets are completely naturalistic and open, and though they are not improvisational, they often appear so because of their exuberance.

These are the moments in *Queen Victoria* that most exhibit words-in-freedom, words free to open new worlds of personal and poetic expression. Here is Wilson's metatheatre at its zenith. Here autism is assigned an aesthetic value; it is to be regarded not as symptomatic of a disturbance but as a comprehensible phenomenon—Knowles' meaningful expression of himself in the world. By finding a creative place for Knowles in his theatre Wilson has challenged psychologists' insistence that the autistic child cannot be integrated into society. He has proposed him as a model member of a new society through his use of the phenomenology of autism as an aesthetic anchor of his theatre; so it seems, since the performers imitate Knowles rather than vice versa.

This coming together of life and art in a new metatheatrical naturalism is not limited to Knowles. For the production of the opera Wilson imported his elderly grandmother from Texas and had her utter words in the Introduction based on her real-life circumstances.

> Q. V.   I HAVE TO TAKE FIVE PILLS A DAY TO
> KEEP ME GOING
> ONE BLOOD PRESSURE PILL
> TWO VITAMIN PILLS AND
> TWO DIABETIC PILLS
> WITHOUT THEM, I'D JUST COLLAPSE

At other times theatricalism is evident in the actors' use of their real names in the text in bold disregard of concepts of character. In Act I, for example, 1 and 2 call each other by first names—and more than a half dozen other names, too. These transformations of character embody the shifting realities of Wilson's theatre, a world where language and speaker metamorphose to suit the poetic demands of the stage.

If the transformation of roles is characteristic of *Queen Victoria* so is the transformation or poetization of stage space. Wilson, who studied architecture and painted early in his career, has turned easily from painting canvases to creating living pictures on the stage. His settings call to mind the early poetic and mystical theatre of Vassily Kandinsky who called his works "stage compositions" and each scene a "stage picture." Like Kandinsky, Wilson creates on stage a landscape of sculptured forms lit by the power of brilliant colors—a visual poetry of transcendent beauty and spirituality.

Peopling this world are Wilson's "ambulant architecture," a term used elsewhere by Bauhaus artist Oscar Schlemmer, which seems the perfect epithet for the performer in *Queen Victoria*. There is not a more distinctive way to describe the image of a woman in a garden, in a flowing white robe pulled to a triangle at her back, or her companion in black, and a black woman, atop a pedestal like some mock Statue of Liberty. Later, when in a play of images, the woman in white takes off her robe and underneath she wears a black dress, while the woman in black takes off hers to expose a white dress—and the two repeat a previous exchange of discourse—it is as though the speeches (and the images) are reversed. Black and white, light and dark, symbolize consciousness and the unconscious, knowledge and lack of knowledge—states of being that Wilson explores thematically. On the social level, black and white symbolize his concerns with themes of racism and justice.

Not only black and white, but color and shape are important in this Theatre of Images: the reds in the murder melodrama of the last act; the stunning yellow that fills the stage and lights up a huge grid at the last line of the Sundance Kid speech; the stroboscopic effect of the Chinaman's speech behind a wooden screen; the blackness of Act II which precedes the brightness of Act III.

In the theatre of Robert Wilson the textures of words resound in space, and space itself is emblazoned with the commingling of man and object in images of splendid disarray. *A Letter for Queen Victoria* is the adventure of the soul from birth to judgment to rebirth, painted in sweeping, opulent strokes on Wilson's living canvas. Perhaps it is a grander vision of life than we are used to. "The point," as Cocteau once wrote, "is not to create life on the stage, but to make the stage live."

BONNIE MARRANCA

PREFACE:
ROBERT WILSON

The Letter

I was thinking about everything when I wrote *A Letter For Queen Victoria*. A letter for Queen Victoria, for instance—what's that? And then Stefan Brecht gave me a letter he had written from a letter somebody actually sent Queen Victoria. I liked it because it was nineteenth-century language:

> ALBEIT IN NO WAY POSSESSED OF THE HONOR OF AN
> INTRODUCTION, AND INDEED INFINITELY REMOVED FROM THE
> DESERVING OF IT, YEA, SINGULARLY UNFIT FOR EXPOSURE TO
> THE BRILLIANCE OF YOUR SUN...A CONDITION SO
> ABJECT...THE SCARCELY FORGIVABLE PRESUMPTION...
> DEPRIVED OF THE LEAST TALENT FOR THE EXERCISE OF
> THE ARTS OF ADDRESS...TO WIT, A DEPRIVATION OF MERIT SO
> ABSOLUTE AS MUST, BY ITS MATHEMATICAL ABSURDITY...

This is all one sentence. I didn't understand any of it but the language interested me; it had changed so quickly in just a century. It was obsolete:

> ...BEFORE EVEN ITS MORAL PARADOX, PUZZLE ONE
> DISCOMMODED INTO THE MOST FLEETING ATTENTION, BUT
> BEING IN A SLIGHT MEASURE (SUFFICIENT TO INDUCE ME TO
> PUT PEN TO PAPER, IF I MAY BE ALLOWED THIS METAPHOR...

I never saw the original so I don't know how Stefan rewrote it. But after all this he added one word:

...ONLY DUE TO THE CULPABLE EXCESS OF MY DESIRE)
ENCOURAGED TO ACT CONTRARILY TO THESE GOOD REASONS
BY MY AWARENESS OF YOUR UNEXCELLED INDULGENCE.
GOOD.

Four characters read the letter as an entr'acte before the opera began.

The Envelope

I like straight lines. Like a rectangle, which is the frame of the stage—you know, those classical proportions. Or like an envelope—it's all straight lines. The letter came later. Before that I was thinking about something I saw and something somebody said.

I had a photograph of Cindy Lubar, taken in the attic of an abbey we were staying in in France, wearing a piece of muslin draped in a triangular shape with a hole cut out for her head. It looked like an envelope. And then on the radio or in the office I heard somebody say:

YOU HAVE A SMUDGE ON YOUR COLLAR.

I wrote that down. And I started thinking, "That's the same shape. If you have a white collar and there's a smudge on it and you framed it, that would be like an envelope with the same diagonal line." We had a little picture frame and we held it towards a white rectangular collar which had a smudge on it and took a slide of it. It was very abstract. And then in the opera we projected it whenever a character repeated the line, "There's a smudge...." It filled the whole stage, tracing the same diagonal line.

The stage was divided into diagonal sections. When the curtain went up, Sheryl Sutton was standing tall upstage left and Cindy Lubar was in front of her downstage right. The line between them traced the same diagonal line continued in Cindy's white dress. Twice in the first act the girls met in the center of the stage, fell over and formed the same diagonal line. In the second act the light coming in through the windows fell in the same diagonal line.

In the fourth act the venetian blinds slant on the same diagonal line. The line was traced or drawn through all the acts. Sometimes it was the costumes, sometimes it was the scenery, sometimes it was the lighting. Sometimes I was not aware of it. I often do things and do not know I have done them until later when I talk about them.

Christopher

I was also thinking about something Christopher Knowles said:

the angle of the thing angling

Christopher was living with me when I was writing *A Letter For Queen Victoria*. We had a *TV* and four radios on all the time. He also had tape recorders going, playing back things that had just occurred. He was making constructions out of what he heard. One page he wrote was very good:

MAD
VERY MAD
VERY VERY MAD
VERY VERY VERY MAD
VERY VERY VERY VERY MAD...

He'd go all the way to the edge of the page and then start over again:

MAD
VERY MAD...

I was interested because it was similar to the way I had been writing in my notebooks. He would write something both for the sound and for the way the words looked on the page. The words looked the way they sounded.

I was thinking about the number four—the four acts, the string quartet and the four characters. I was not thinking about the characters as different people. They sound like four different people yet they all sound the same. I never had to explain anything to Christopher because he'd just take what I was doing and use it for his own purposes. When I started numbering people in the script—character 1, character 2, character 3 and character 4—he picked up on it and did the same thing. "The angle of the thing..." was the first line of dialogue I picked up from him although it's the last line of the opera.

The Opera

The lowest part of the stage, downstage, was like a dead zone where nobody went, like a frame around the edge. There were brightly lit objects there in front of every act—a tank of water, an electric heater, a head of lettuce and a rock. Behind this the string quartet played continuously. I amplified the almost whisper dialogue so the characters could be heard with the music without unnecessary effort. When two characters would speak at once, they didn't have to drown each other out.

People say that people do not act in my work but I think they do. We rehearsed the dialogue over and over again so that it became mechanical. People could almost do it in their sleep. But by repeating dialogue over and over again you become more careful about what you're saying and what you're feeling when you say it. You also become more aware of what somebody else is saying and feeling at the same time.

People can do several things at once. We can watch television and follow the story, we can talk to somebody on the telephone and also talk to somebody sitting across from us who's talking to somebody else. I called *A Letter For Queen Victoria* an "opera" because everything in it happens at once, the way it does in operas and the way it does in life.

ROBERT WILSON
REDACTED BY CHRISTOPHER HEMPHILL

A Letter For Queen Victoria had its premiere on June 15, 1974 in Spoleto, Italy at the Festival of Two Worlds. The production opened on Broadway at the A.N.T.A. Theatre on March 22, 1975. It was written, directed and designed by Robert Wilson. The BYRD HOFFMAN FOUNDATION presented it in New York.

Cast . . . . . . George Ashley, Stefan Brecht, Katryn Cation, Alma Hamilton, Christopher Knowles, Cynthia Lubar, James Neu, Scotty Snyder, Sheryl Sutton, Robert Wilson

Music . . Alan Lloyd in collaboration with Michael Galasso

Musical Direction . . . . Michael Galasso

Musicians . . . . Kevin Byrnes, Kathryn Cation, Laura Epstein, Michael Galasso, Susan Krongold

Choreography . . . . Andrew deGroat

Dancers . . . . Andrew deGroat, Julia Busto

Scenery and Costume Supervision . . . . Peter Harvey

Lighting Supervision . . . . . . Beverly Emmons, assisted by Carol Mullins

Slides . . . . Francis Brooks

Verbal Tape Constructions . . . . Christopher Knowles

Introductory Letter . . . . Stefan Brecht

The Sundance Kid Speech . . . . Christopher Knowles

Act III Dialogue . . . . Cynthia Lubar

1st Speech of Chinaman . . . . James Neu

Entr'actes are by Christopher Knowles and Robert Wilson.

A LETTER FOR
QUEEN VICTORIA

INTRODUCTION

1
2
3
4

ACT I

1	1		1	1
2	2		2	2
PILOTS	PILOTS		WARDEN	1A
	BILLY			2A
				BILLY
				CHRIS
				PILOT

ACT II

1	1		1	1
2	2		2	2
3	3		3	3
4	4		4	4
WARDEN	WARDEN		CIVIL WAR SOLDIER	CHRIS
	CHRIS		JIM	

ACT III

	1C			1B	
1D	2C	1E		2B	1A
2D		2E			2A

51

ACT IV

1	1	1	1
2	2	2	2
2A	2A	2A	PILOTS
3	3	3	
4	4	4	
BILLY	BILLY	BILLY	
		CHRIS	

INTRODUCTION

(WHEN AUDIENCE ENTERS THE THEATRE THE DANCERS ARE SPINNING ON THE FORESTAGE, MUSIC IS PLAYING, AND QUEEN VICTORIA STANDS BEFORE SHOW CURTAIN.)* (CHRISTOPHER KNOWLES READS HIS LETTER, AND THREE MEMBERS OF THE CAST SIMULTANEOUSLY READ THE OTHER LETTER.)

DEAR MADAM,
MOST GRACIOUS OF LADIES,
AUGUST IMPERATRICE,

ALBEIT IN NO WAY POSSESSED OF THE HONOR OF AN INTRODUCTION AND INDEED INFINITELY REMOVED FROM THE DESERVING OF IT YEA SINGULARLY FOR THE UNFIT FOR THE EXPOSURE TO THE BRILLIANCE OF YOUR SUN BEING IN VERY OF THE DISNEYSORE OF IT IS ITS DESTITU-TION OF GRACE, OUTWARD OR INWARD, AS TO MAKE MY PRESENCE TOLER-RABLE ONLY TO THE HUMBLEST ABOUNDING IN THE BOUNTY OF TOLERANCE, I HAVE THE SCARCELY FORGIVA-BLE OF THE PRESUMPTION OF ADDRESSING MYSELF TO YOU, KNOWING FULWELL THE DISPOS-ISORE OF THIS MERIT OF THIS POSITAL OF OF THAT IN IN IN INTO THE SPOTLESS LIGHTS AND THEN WE AND THEN AND THEN ABOUT THE UM THE UMMM ABOUT THE MOST FLEETING ATTENTION AND ABOUT ABOUT THE ABOUT THE TREES IN IN THE WOODS IN IN IN IN WHERES WHERE WHERE IT IS TO DO THE EXERCISE OF OF THE ADDRESSING KN-KNOWING FULWELL AND THEN SOMETHING IT IS, OF THE PARADISE,PUZZLE OF THE PARADISE.   GOOD.

SOME TEN YEARS AGO A STROKE OF ILL FORTUNE ATTACHED TO MY VACUOUS OCCUPIED RACING AND TO TO THE MUNICIPAL FIXTURE AND AND ONLY TO THE HUMBLEST ABOUNDING IN IN IN IN ONES WHERE IT IS IT IS AND THAT IT IT ITS IT'S THE IT'S THE UMM THE UMMMMM OF OF THIS DISTRACTION AND ABOUT ABOUT THE MAN'S LATE MORNING SHADOW TO EVERY SIDE OF IT AND ALSO I AS I'S AS I ADD AS I MUST TO DO JUSTICE TO THE FACTS AAAND AND AND THEN AND THEN WE AND THEN UMM AN AND THEN AND THEN ABOUT ABOUT THE OF OF OF THIS NOT—DON'T LET THAT POST STAND IN SPACE AND THEN ABOUT AWHILE AGO IT COULD BE IN THE ONE NOBODY ELSE WAS NOT HURT, PUT THE MAT PUT THE MATTER BRIEFLY TEN YEARS OF A RESEARCH OF OF A DIS DISPARADISE AND THEN WE HAVE SOMETHING OF THIS IS THAN MORE THE M MORE THAN AN ANY NARY A THING WHOLLY DEPRIVED OF OF A DIS-NEYSORC3JET AND OF THIS PILOT OF OF DISTRACTION ANDZUP AND THE UM AND I AND AND ABOUT THE UM A ABOUT THE PLACES WHAT HAS BEEN ITS WAS SUCH A CRUDE IN THE ONE SEE WHAT IT IS AND ABOUT THE UM SINGULARLY THEN, ABOUT WHAT IT IS AND ABOUT THE UM THE THE ONES IT COULD BE AND PERSONALLY IT IS ON ON YOURSELF WHOSE HUMBLE AND OF OF THE MAJESTY'S AND ALL THAT, WHOSE WATCHBOA AND ABOUT THEN AND WHO

HUMBLE WHOSE HUMBLE AND OBEDIENT SERVANT I BEG TO BE ALLOWED TO CONFIRM MYSELF TO BE.

RUFUS SMITH

*THE SHOW CURTAIN USED THROUGHOUT THE PRODUCTION IS PRINTED ON PAGE 108 OF TEXT.

(CHRISTOPHER KNOWLES' VERSION OF STEFAN BRECHT'S INTRODUCTORY LETTER)

DEAR MADAM,
MOST GRACIOUS OF LADIES,
AUGUST IMPERATRICE:

ALBEIT IN NO WAY POSSESSED OF THE HONOR OF AN INTRODUCTION, AND INDEED INFINITELY REMOVED FROM THE DESERVING OF IT, YEA, SINGULARLY UNFIT FOR EXPOSURE TO THE BRILLIANCE OF YOUR SUN, BEING IN VERITY OF A CONDITION SO ABJECT IN ITS DESTITUTION OF GRACE, OUTWARD OR INWARD, AS TO MAKE MY PRESENCE TOLERABLE ONLY TO THE HUMBLEST ABOUNDING IN THE BOUNTY OF TOLERANCE, I HAVE THE SCARCELY FORGIVABLE PRESUMPTION OF ADDRESSING MYSELF TO YOU, KNOWING FULWELL THE POSITIVE DISMERIT HEREOF ON THE PART OF ONE NOT ONLY DEPRIVED OF THE LEAST TALENT FOR THE EXERCISE OF THE ARTS OF ADDRESS BUT HAVING THE BEST REASONS TO FEAR NOTICE, TO WIT A DEPRIVATION OF MERIT SO ABSOLUTE AS MUST, BY ITS MATHEMATICAL ABSURDITY, BEFORE EVEN ITS MORAL PARADOX, PUZZLE ONE DISCOMMODED INTO THE MOST FLEETING ATTENTION, BUT BEING IN A SLIGHT MEASURE (SUFFICIENT TO INDUCE ME TO PUT PEN TO PAPER, IF I MAY BE ALLOWED THIS METAPHOR, ONLY DUE TO THE CULPABLE EXCESS OF MY DESIRE) ENCOURAGED TO ACT CONTRARILY TO THESE GOOD REASONS BY MY AWARENESS OF YOUR UNEXCELLED INDULGENCE.   GOOD.

SOME TEN YEARS AGO A STROKE OF ILL FORTUNE ATTACHED MY VACCUOUSLY PREOCCUPIED GAZE TO A MUNICIPAL FIXTURE IMMURED IN THE CURB OF A SMALL DEADEND SIDE STREET PERPENDICULAR TO THE THOROUGHFARE ALONG WHICH, SEATED ON A STREETCAR, I WAS PASSING. IT WAS AN UNLIT STREET LAMP. TO MY LASTING AMAZEMENT, THE UNDISTINGUISHED POST, NO SOONER SEEN BY ME THAN PASSED OUT OF SIGHT, STOOD IN SOVEREIGNTY IN A SMALL BUT WELL-DEFINED INFINITY, EXTENDING PERHAPS THE EXTENT OF A MAN'S LATE MORNING SHADOW TO EVERY SIDE OF IT. SO FAR THE MATTER MAY NOT SEEM OF EXCESSIVE CURIOSITY TO THE NOMINALIST, BUT IF I ADD, AS I MUST TO DO JUSTICE TO THE FACTS, THAT THIS SPACE OF INFINITY WAS TEMPORAL IN NATURE, I FEAR THAT I SHALL STRAIN THE CREDULITY OF THE MOST COMPLAISANT. FOR DID NOT THIS POST STAND IN SPACE AND DID I NOT SEE IT FOR BUT A SECOND? NEVERTHELESS, THIS MUCH WAS PLAIN TO MY SENSES. TO PUT THE MATTER BRIEFLY, TEN YEARS OF RESEARCH HAVE DISCLOSED TO ME NOT ONLY THE EXISTENCE OF A NUMBER OF SUCH INCURSIONS OF ETERNITY WITHIN THE CONFINES OF YOUR MAJESTY'S CAPITAL & DOMINIONS HERE & THERE, AND I APPEND A LIST, BUT THAT, PROVIDED ONE'S ATTENTION BE UNDISTRACTED, THERE IS NARY A THING WHOLLY DEPRIVED OF THE MAJESTY OF SUCH A RESIDENCE, SO NEARLY CONSISTENTLY SO, THAT I HAVE BEEN LEAD TO ENTERTAIN THE HYPOTHESIS, SO FAR NO MORE THAN AN HYPOTHESIS, THAT THE APPEARANCE OF TEMPORAL DEFINITION WITHIN SPACE IS BUT THE PRODUCT OF DISTRACTION. I NEED NOT, I AM SURE, ADDUCE THE DISQUIETING IMPLICATIONS OF MY

DISCOVERY TO ONE AS ACCUTE & INFORMED AS YOUR MAJESTY, WHOSE HUMBLE & OBE-
DIENT SERVANT I BEG TO BE ALLOWED TO CONFIRM MYSELF TO BE.

RUFUS SMITH

(ROBERT WILSON AND CHRISTOPHER KNOWLES SPEAK)
1 A
2 B
1 A
2 B
1 ABABABABAB
2 ABABABAB AB   B
1   A   A   AAAAABBB
2   B   B   BBBBBAAA
1 A   LADIES AND GENTLE
2 (LONG PAUSE) MEN
1 A LETTER FOR QUEEN   A
2 (LONG PAUSE) B
1 VICTORIA   A
2 B
1 WHAT ARE WE DOING
2 WE'RE DOING THE FOUR ACTS   ACT ONE ACT TWO ACT THREE AND ACT FOUR
1 WHAT ARE WE DOING   A
2 WE'RE DOING THE PLAY
1 WHAT ARE WE DOING   A
2 WE'RE DOING "A LETTER FOR QUEEN VICTORIA"   B
1 WHAT ARE WE DOING
2 WE'RE DOING THE FOUR ACTS
1 WHERE ARE WE
2 WE ARE IN THE THEATRE
1 WHERE ARE WE   A
2 B   WE ARE IN NEW YORK
1 WHERE ARE WE
2 WE ARE AT THE THEATRE IN MANHATTAN
                 IN NEW YORK
                 IN THE WORLD
                 IN THE WORLD
                 IN THE WORLD
                 IN THE WORLD
(1, 2, 3, 4, TIPTOE STAGE RIGHT; EXIT)
QUEEN VICTORIA: I HAVE TO TAKE FIVE PILLS A DAY TO KEEP ME GOING
                 ONE BLOOD PRESSURE PILL
                 TWO VITAMIN PILLS AND
                 TWO DIABETIC PILLS
                 WITHOUT THEM, I'D JUST COLLAPSE
(QUEEN VICTORIA SLOWLY RAISES ARMS AND SCREAMS THREE TIMES.
END OF INTRODUCTION.)

ACT I
SECTION 1

(CURTAIN UP)

1 (SCREAM SONG)
2 (SCREAM SONG)

1 SHE BROKE HER NECK
2 THAT'S NOT WHAT I DID

1 OH YOU WERE
2 THANK YOU

1 YEAH WELL THAT STUFF
2 WERE THEY WERE THEY A . . . YEAH I KNOW

1 HAVE YOU BEEN HERE BEFORE?
2 NO, THIS IS THE FIRST TIME . . . OK, THANK YOU VERY MUCH

1 HAVE YOU BEEN HERE BEFORE?
2 NO, THIS IS THE FIRST TIME . . . OK, THANK YOU VERY MUCH

1 NO, GRACE, YOU NEVER HAVE TOLD ME ABOUT IT BUT SOMEDAY YOU MUST

2 NO, I HAVE NEVER HANDLED A PROBATE CASE, I'VE TOLD YOU THAT

1 THANK YOU GRACE   I MEAN YOU'RE NOT A COOK . . . YOU
2 I MEAN I COME HOME FROM WORK AND EXPECT A MEAL ON THE TABLE I MEAN A MAN IS A
   WOMAN

1 SHE RESENTS IT
2 OH, THAT'S A PROBLEM

1 SO WHAT IF SHE DID
2 YOU MUST NOT TELL MANDA IT HER BIRTHDAY PLEASE DON'T TELL ADAM

1 MANDA SHE LOVE A GOOD JOKE YOU KNOW. SHE A LAWYER TOO.
2 LET'S WASH SOME DISHES.

1 WHAT DO YOU DO MY DEAR?
2 OH, SHE'S A SOCIAL WORKER

1 NICE TRY GRACE
2 MANDA, THERE ARE NO ACCIDENTS

1 I'M SORRY   IT SURE IS HOT OUT
2 IT'S HOTTER IN HERE

1   FIREHOUSE AND THE MEN WHO FIGHT THEM
2   WHAT??

1   DON'T MAKE ME KILL YOU
2   JIM, JIM, JIM!!!

1   I'M SORRY ROSE
2   YOU KILLED HIM   YOU KILLED MY BROTHER

1   I'M SORRY ROSE
2   YOU KILLED MY BROTHER AND WHAT'S BETWEEN. I HATE YOU.

1   I GUESS YOU'RE RIGHT—WE LIVE IN TWO DIFFERENT WORLDS YOU AND I DO
                                                                    I DO
2   I FORGIVE MY SON—HE DOES NOT KNOW WHAT HE HAS DONE

1   YOU BETTER FIT RUNNING THE RANCH
2   WELCOME HOME BEN

1   NOW THAT YOU'RE HOME I GUESS YOU'LL WANT YOUR OLD THINGS BACK

2   WELL THE WAR'S OVER I GUESS THE YANKEES WILL JUST HAVE TO LEARN

1   GOOD. I'LL DRINK TO THAT.
2   I JUST NEVER SAW ANYTHING LIKE IT IN MY LIFE

1   IT WAS A SLAUGHTER
2   NOW I DON'T BELIEVE THAT, JOHN.

1   I DIDN'T SAY A WORD ABOUT COWARDS
2   HA HA ARE YOU GOING CRAZY

1   IT DOESN'T MEAN
2   HA HA   I GUESS THERE'S NO ARGUMENT AS TO WHO WON THAT ARGUMENT

1   BEN GOT HIMSELF A MEDAL
2   HE JUST TALKING BIG

1   ANYONE WANT TO MAKE IT HIS BUSINESS
2   I GUESS TIME DOESN'T NEED YOU TO PROTECT IT

1   I STOPPED AT THE STATION BECAUSE IT WAS RAINING
2   I GUESS YOU'RE WRONG

1   YOU MEAN YOU WON'T QUIT
2   MOST PEOPLE IN THIS TOWN ARE REAL AGREEABLE

1   NO YANKEE IS GOING TO BE A NEIGHBOR OF MINE
2   THIS TOWN NEEDS YOU

1 SOME UNION SOLDIER JUST CAME INTO TOWN
2 THE ARMY IS SETTING UP A PORT TWENTY MILES FROM THIS TOWN

1 TROUBLE WITH YOU FOLKS IS THAT YOU'RE STILL LIVING IN THE PAST PAST IS THERE A
   LOT OF IT LEFT?
2 THEY'RE TAKING OUT ALL OF THE RICH DEPOSITS—THEY'RE TAKING AWAY THE
   VEGETATION—THEY'RE FIXING IT UP. I WORK FOR AL CAMP. IT'S JUST MIXING ALL MUD.

1 WHY DO THEY JUST PUT IT ALL OUT IN THE COUNTRY
2 WHEN THEY EVENTUALLY ABANDON THE AREA IT JUST GETS ALL SOLID—ONCE YOU START
   LIMITING THE QUANTITY OF IT ALL . . .

1 I REMEMBER AFTER THE WAR I MET THIS GUY WHO WAS WORKING FOR HIS WIFE.
2 BAM! WOW! THE BRITISH ARE VERY CONSERVATIVE.

1 THEY EAT THIS FAT TO KEEP YOU WARM. IT MAKES SENSE.
2 THEY'VE GONE COMPLETELY MUCKY BUCKY–OO (SUNG)–ABOUT IT

1 WELL IT'S VERY DIFFERENT. IT'S NOT THAT POPULAR HERE.
2 WELL YOU UNDERSTAND THE BASIC GAME   ONE EAR UP AND ONE EAR DOWN.

1 SEND ME—GET THEE BACK O CROCODILE THAT DWELLEST IN THE EAST—DOWN A ROPE
2 OK

1 HELLO MISTER. WANT ANY SAUCE, WANT ANY SALT, WANT ANY LIQUOR. NO? WELL, GOOD
   DAY.
2 WELL WE HAVE TO HAVE SOME PLACE TO KEEP OUR POPSICLES.

1 SURE IS HOT IN HERE
2 OUTSIDE IT'S 40°

1 IN OUR CASE WE CREATE A CRUST GRID—BUT IT WILL WORK
2 HM HM HM <u>HM</u>

1 THEY'VE HAD ICE MAKING MACHINES AROUND FOR A LONG TIME. YOU CAN'T WIN THEM
   ALL MAN.
2 MANDY YOU JUST GOT MARRIED.

1 MANDY I GOT A GET A DIVORCE.
2 MANDY IT JUST NOT HUMAN.

1 I GOTTA A DIVORCE. I CAN'T BELIEVE YOU ARE A LAWYER'S ASSISTANT.
2 DON'T YOU KNOW THAT'S IPSICK
                         DIPSICK   IT'S LATIN. IT DOESN'T MEAN A THING.

1 I DON'T BELIEVE YOU
2 OH, YOU HAVE A SMUDGE ON YOUR COLLAR

1 THIS ACT WAS DELIBERATE AND PROVOKED

2   HE TOLD ME SOME DAY HE'D GET EVEN

1   THIS ACT WAS DELIBERATE AND PROVOKED
2   HE TOLD ME SOME DAY HE'D GET EVEN

1   YOUR HONOR   IPSICK DIPSICK
2   IF YOU CAN'T CONTAIN THAT GIRL DON'T BRING HER BACK

1   HMM HMM HMM
2   IF THIS CASE PAYS OFF THEN ON TO THE BIG TIME

1   I SUPPOSE A REENACTMENT OF THE CASE IS NECESSARY
2   YOU KNOW THAT EXPERIENCE IN COURT WOULD MAKE A GOOD MOVIE

1   AND THEY WOULD CALL CLANTON KLUX
2   NEXT...

1   I DON'T WANT TO GIVE AWAY THE PLOT—IT'S ABOUT A PLANECRASH AND PILOT—IT LIKE
    TRYING NOT TO RETIRE AND DIE IN BED IN CHINA. SUPPOSE THERE WAS A PLANECRASH
    AND EVERYONE DIED BUT THE PILOT.

(TWO PILOTS ENTER)
PILOT: TAKE THIS STONE AWAY. I WANT YOU JUST THE WAY YOU ARE.

2   I KNOW ABOUT THAT

1   I SUPPOSE WHILE YOU'RE WRITING
2   IT'S ELEVEN O'CLOCK.

1   THERE THEY ARE.
2   WHAT TIME FRIDAY?

1   THIS HOUSE IS FULL OF MIDNIGHT REEFER.
2   EITHER WAY UNCLE BRINKLEY, DON'T YOU THINK I'M OLD ENOUGH TO OPEN THE DOOR.

1   GOOD NIGHT, MR. GRAY.
2   HE SURE PLAYS MEAN MAMBO.

1   I FORGOT MY KEY AGAIN.
2   SEE YOU AROUND? !!!

1   DO YOU KNOW WHAT THAT MEANS.
2   THE KISS OF DEATH.

1   ALL RIGHT—IF HE'S READY TO SUPPORT AN OLD MAID
2   IT WAS AWFULLY NICE OF YOU TO COME OUT

1   HE TWICE AS DANGEROUS AS I WAS
2   ALRIGHT I GET IT—OK. SO GIRLS LIKE DANGEROUS BOYS.

1   ANOTHER THING THAT LAKE OUT BACK WE CALL A SWIMMING POOL.
2   DON'T WORRY. I WOULD LET YOU STAY HERE ALONE.

1   WHY DON'T I LET YOU IN.

(PILOTS EXIT)

1   I'VE BEEN TAKING SOME LESSONS FROM A BOY THAT I KNOW. JUSTICE SHOULD BE HEARD
EQUALLY. LA JUSTICE DEVRAIT ÊTRE ENTENDU ÉGALEMENT.

    (CHARACTER 1 STEPS FORWARD, STEPS ON AN ALLIGATOR, AND THE ALLIGATOR BITES 1's
    FOOT—SHE PICKS UP FOOT TO TAKE ALLIGATOR OFF)

ACT I
SECTION 2

(BREAK DROP DOWN. ROBERT WILSON ON SIDE OF STAGE IN FRONT OF LIGHT BREAK DROP
PAINTED AS A DAM. HE SCRATCHES HEAD.)

(DURING BREAK DROP IN ACT I)

ROBERT: PIRUP   PIRUP

(TAPE OF CHRISTOPHER SOUNDS FROM OFF-STAGE):
                            PIRUP   PIRUP   PIRUP
                            PIRUP   PIRUP   PIRUP
                            PIRUP   PIRUP   PIRUP
                            PIRUP   PIRUP   PIRUP
                            PIRUP   PIRUP   PIRUP
                            PIRUP   PIRUP   PIRUP
                            PIRUP   PIRUP   PIRUP
(BREAK DROP UP)

2   HI SHERYL, HOW ARE YOU?
1   OK

2   DO YOU WANT TO WALK IN THE GARDEN?
1   OK

1   HI CINDY, HOW ARE YOU?
2   OK

1   DO YOU WANT TO WALK IN THE GARDEN?
2   OK

(1 & 2 BEND OVER TOGETHER, THERE IS THE SOUND OF AN EXPLOSION AND A SLIDE OF THE
ATOMIC BOMB BLAST)

1   SHE BROKE HER NECK
2   THAT'S NOT WHAT I DID

1   OH YOU WERE
2   THANK YOU

1   YEAH WELL THAT STUFF
2   WERE THEY   WERE THEY A . . . YEAH I KNOW

1   HAVE YOU BEEN HERE BEFORE?
2   NO, THIS IS THE FIRST TIME . . . OK, THANK YOU VERY MUCH.

1   HAVE YOU BEEN HERE BEFORE?
2   NO, THIS IS THE FIRST TIME . . . OK, THANK YOU VERY MUCH.

1   NO GRACE, YOU NEVER HAVE TOLD ME ABOUT IT BUT SOMEDAY YOU MUST.

2   NO, I HAVE NEVER HANDLED A PROBATE CASE, I'VE TOLD YOU THAT.

1   THANK YOU GRACE I MEAN YOU'RE NOT A COOK . . . YOU
2   I MEAN I COME HOME FROM WORK AND EXPECT A MEAL ON THE TABLE.
    I MEAN A MAN IS A WOMAN.

1   SHE RESENTS IT.
2   OH, THAT THAT THAT'S A PROBLEM.

1   SO WHAT IF SHE DID
2   YOU MUST NOT TELL MANDA IT HER BIRTHDAY   PLEASE DON'T TELL ADAM

1   MANDA SHE LOVE A GOOD JOKE YOU KNOW. SHE A LAWYER TOO.
2   LET'S WASH SOME DISHES.

1   WHAT DO YOU DO MY DEAR?
2   OH, SHE'S A SOCIAL WORKER

1   NICE TRY GRACE
2   MANDA THERE ARE NO ACCIDENTS

1   I'M SORRY   IT SURE IS HOT OUT
2   IT'S HOTTER IN HERE

1   FIREHOUSE AND THE MEN WHO FIGHT THEM
2   WHAT??

1   DON'T MAKE ME KILL YOU
2   JIM, JIM, JIM!!!

1   I'M SORRY ROSE
2   YOU KILLED HIM   YOU KILLED MY BROTHER

1   I'M SORRY ROSE
2   YOU KILLED MY BROTHER AND WHAT'S BETWEEN. I HATE YOU.

1   I GUESS YOU'RE RIGHT—WE LIVE IN TWO DIFFERENT WORLDS YOU AND I DO
                                                           I DO
                              (I AND 2 SCREAM)
2   I FORGIVE MY SON—HE DOES NOT KNOW WHAT HE HAS DONE

1   YOU BETTER FIT RUNNING THE RANCH
2   WELCOME HOME BEN

1   NOW THAT YOU'RE HOME I GUESS YOU'LL WANT YOUR OLD THINGS BACK

2   WELL THE WAR IS OVER   I GUESS THE YANKEES WILL JUST HAVE TO LEARN

1   GOOD. I'LL DRINK TO THAT.
2   I JUST NEVER SAW ANYTHING LIKE IT IN MY LIFE

1   IT WAS A SLAUGHTER.
2   NOW I DON'T BELIEVE THAT, JOHN.

1   I DIDN'T SAY A WORD ABOUT COWARDS
2   HA HA ARE YOU GOING CRAZY

1   IT DOESN'T MEAN
2   HA HA I GUESS THERE'S NO ARGUMENT AS TO WHO WON THAT ARGUMENT

1   BEN GOT HIMSELF A MEDAL
2   HE JUST TALKING BIG

1   ANYONE WANT TO MAKE IT HIS BUSINESS
2   I GUESS TIME DOESN'T NEED YOU TO PROTECT IT

1   I STOPPED AT THE STATION BECAUSE IT WAS RAINING
2   I GUESS YOU'RE WRONG

1   YOU MEAN YOU WON'T QUIT
2   MOST PEOPLE IN THIS TOWN ARE REAL AGREEABLE

1   NO YANKEE IS GOING TO BE A NEIGHBOR OF MINE
2   THIS TOWN NEEDS YOU

1   SOME UNION SOLDIER JUST CAME INTO TOWN
2   THE ARMY IS SETTING UP A PORT TWENTY MILES FROM THIS TOWN

1   TROUBLE WITH YOU FOLKS IS THAT YOU'RE STILL LIVING IN THE PAST PAST   IS THERE A
    LOT OF IT LEFT?
2   THEY'RE TAKING OUT ALL OF THE RICH DEPOSITS—THEY'RE TAKING AWAY ALL THE
    VEGETATION—THEY'RE FIXING IT UP. I WORK FOR AL CAMP. IT'S JUST MIXING ALL MUD.

1   WHY DO THEY JUST PUT IT ALL OUT IN THE COUNTRY.
2   WHEN THEY EVENTUALLY ABANDON THE AREA IT JUST GETS ALL SOLID, ONCE YOU START LIMITING THE QUANTITY OF IT ALL . . .

1   I REMEMBER AFTER THE WAR I MET THIS GUY WHO WAS WORKING FOR HIS WIFE.

2   BAM! WOW! THE BRITISH ARE VERY CONSERVATIVE.

1   THEY EAT THIS FAT TO KEEP YOU WARM. IT MAKES SENSE.
2   THEY'VE GONE COMPLETELY MUCKY BUCKY–OOH–ABOUT IT.

1   WELL IT'S VERY DIFFERENT. IT'S NOT THAT POPULAR HERE.
2   WELL YOU UNDERSTAND THE BASIC GAME ONE EAR UP AND ONE EAR DOWN.

1   SEND ME—GET THEE BACK O CROCODILE THAT DWELLEST IN THE EAST—IS THAT RIGHT—EAST?—DOWN A ROPE
2   OK

1   HELLO MISTER. WANT ANY SAUCE, WANT ANY SALT, WANT ANY LIQUOR. NO? WELL GOOD DAY.
2   WELL WE HAVE TO HAVE SOME PLACE TO KEEP OUR POPSICLES.

1   SURE IS HOT IN HERE
2   OUTSIDE IT'S 40°

1   IN OUR CASE WE CREATE A CRUST GRID—BUT IT WILL WORK

2   HM HM HM <u>HM</u>

1   THEY'VE HAD ICE MAKING MACHINES AROUND FOR A LONG TIME. YOU CAN'T WIN THEM ALL MAN.
2   MANDY YOU JUST GOT MARRIED.

1   MANDY I GOT A GET A DIVORCE.
2   MANDY IT JUST NOT HUMAN.

1   I GOTTA A DIVORCE. I CAN'T BELIEVE YOU ARE A LAWYER'S ASSISTANT.

2   DON'T YOU KNOW THAT'S IPSICK
                    DIPSICK   IT'S LATIN. IT DOESN'T MEAN A THING.

1   I DON'T BELIEVE YOU.
2   OH, YOU HAVE A SMUDGE ON YOUR COLLAR.

(2 WALKS TO 1, HOLDS SMALL PICTURE FRAME TO 1's COLLAR)
                                        (SLIDE OF SMUDGE ON COLLAR)
2   THE STILL.

1   THIS ACT WAS DELIBERATE AND PROVOKED
2   HE TOLD ME SOME DAY HE'D GET EVEN

1   THIS ACT WAS DELIBERATE AND PROVOKED
2   HE TOLD ME SOME DAY HE'D GET EVEN

1   YOUR HONOR IPSICK DIPSICK
2   IF YOU CAN'T CONTAIN THAT GIRL DON'T BRING HER BACK

1   HMM HMM HMM
2   IF THIS CASE PAYS OFF THEN ON TO THE BIG TIME

1   I SUPPOSE A REENACTMENT OF THE CASE IS NECESSARY
2   YOU KNOW THAT EXPERIENCE IN COURT WOULD MAKE A GOOD MOVIE

1   AND THEY WOULD CALL CLANTON KLUX
2   NEXT . . .

1   I DON'T WANT TO GIVE AWAY THE PLOT—IT'S ABOUT A PLANECRASH AND PILOT—IT'S
    LIKE TRYING NOT TO RETIRE AND DIE IN BED IN CHINA. SUPPOSE THERE WAS A PLANE-
    CRASH AND EVERYONE DIED BUT THE PILOT.

(BILLY, THE GARDENER, ENTERS WITH HEDGE CLIPPERS)
(TWO PILOTS ENTER)

PILOT A: BILLY. BILLY. (TO GARDENER)
PILOT B: EXCUSE ME.
(PILOTS EXIT)

2   I KNOW ABOUT THAT

1   I SUPPOSE WHILE YOU'RE WRITING
2   IT'S ELEVEN O'CLOCK

1   THERE THEY ARE
2   WHAT TIME FRIDAY?

1   THIS HOUSE IS FULL OF MIDNIGHT REEFER.
2   EITHER WAY UNCLE BRINKLEY, DON'T YOU THINK I'M OLD ENOUGH TO OPEN THE DOOR.

1   GOOD NIGHT, MR. GRAY.
2   HE SURE PLAYS MEAN MAMBO.

1   I FORGOT MY KEY AGAIN.
2   SEE YOU AROUND?!!!

1   DO YOU KNOW WHAT THAT MEANS.
2   THE KISS OF DEATH

1   ALL RIGHT—IF HE'S READY TO SUPPORT AN OLD MAID
2   IT WAS AWFULLY NICE OF YOU TO COME OUT

1   HE TWICE AS DANGEROUS AS I WAS

2   ALRIGHT I GET IT—OK. SO GIRLS LIKE DANGEROUS BOYS.

1   ANOTHER THING THAT LAKE OUT BACK THAT WE CALL A SWIMMING POOL
2   DON'T WORRY. I WOULD LET YOU STAY HERE ALONE.

1   WHY DON'T I LET YOU IN. I'VE BEEN TAKING SOME LESSONS FROM A BOY THAT I KNOW.

(1 STEPS FORWARD TOWARDS ALLIGATOR, RAISES FOOT NEAR ALLIGATOR'S MOUTH)

LIGHTS OUT)

ACT I
SECTION 3

(LIGHTS UP)

1   SHE BROKE HER NECK
2   THAT'S NOT WHAT I DID

1   OH YOU WERE
2   THANK YOU

1   YEAH WELL THAT STUFF
2   WERE THEY WERE THEY A . . . YEAH I KNOW

1   HAVE YOU BEEN HERE BEFORE?
2   NO, THIS IS THE FIRST TIME . . . OK, THANK YOU VERY MUCH.

1   HAVE YOU BEEN HERE BEFORE?
2   NO, THIS IS THE FIRST TIME . . . OK, THANK YOU VERY MUCH.

1   NO GRACE, YOU NEVER HAVE TOLD ME ABOUT IT BUT SOME DAY YOU MUST.

2   NO, I HAVE NEVER HANDLED A PROBATE CASE, I'VE TOLD YOU THAT.

1   THANK YOU GRACE   I MEAN YOU'RE NOT A COOK . . . YOU
2   I MEAN I COME HOME FROM WORK AND EXPECT A MEAL ON THE TABLE. I MEAN A MAN IS
     A WOMAN.

1   SHE RESENTS IT.
2   OH, THAT'S A PROBLEM.

1   SO WHAT IF SHE DID.
2   YOU MUST NOT TELL MANDA IT HER BIRTHDAY PLEASE DON'T TELL ADAM

1   MANDA SHE LOVE A GOOD JOKE YOU KNOW. SHE A LAWYER TOO.
2   LET'S WASH SOME DISHES.

1   WHAT DO YOU DO MY DEAR?
2   OH, SHE'S A SOCIAL WORKER.

1   NICE TRY GRACE
2   MANDA THERE ARE NO ACCIDENTS

1   I'M SORRY   IT SURE IS HOT OUT
2   IT'S HOTTER IN HERE

1   FIREHOUSE AND THE MEN WHO FIGHT THEM
2   WHAT??

1   DON'T MAKE ME KILL YOU
2   JIM, JIM, JIM!!!

1   I'M SORRY ROSE
2   YOU KILLED HIM   YOU KILLED MY BROTHER

1   I'M SORRY ROSE
2   YOU KILLED MY BROTHER AND WHAT'S BETWEEN. I HATE YOU.

1   I GUESS YOU'RE RIGHT—WE LIVE IN TWO DIFFERENT WORLDS YOU AND I DO
                                                                    I DO

2   I FORGIVE MY SON—HE DOES NOT KNOW WHAT HE HAS DONE

1   YOU BETTER FIT RUNNING THE RANCH
2   WELL THE WAR'S OVER I GUESS THE YANKEES WILL JUST HAVE TO LEARN.

1   GOOD. I'LL DRINK TO THAT.
2   I JUST NEVER SAW ANYTHING LIKE IT IN MY LIFE

1   IT WAS A SLAUGHTER
2   NOW I DON'T BELIEVE THAT JOHN.

1   I DIDN'T SAY A WORD ABOUT COWARDS
2   HA HA ARE YOU GOING CRAZY

1   IT DOESN'T MEAN
2   HA HA   I GUESS THERE'S NO ARGUMENT AS TO WHO WON THAT ARGUMENT

1   BEN GOT HIMSELF A MEDAL
2   HE JUST TALKING BIG

1   I CAN'T BELIEVE YOU ARE A LAWYER'S ASSISTANT
2   DON'T YOU KNOW THAT'S IPSICK
                           DIPSICK   IT'S LATIN. IT DOESN'T MEAN A THING.

1   I DON'T BELIEVE YOU
2   OH, YOU HAVE A SMUDGE ON YOUR COLLAR.

1   THIS ACT WAS DELIBERATE AND PROVOKED
2   HE TOLD ME SOMEDAY HE'D GET EVEN

1   THIS ACT WAS DELIBERATE AND PROVOKED
2   HE TOLD ME SOME DAY HE'D GET EVEN

1   YOUR HONOR IPSICK DIPSICK
2   IF YOU CAN'T CONTAIN THAT GIRL DON'T BRING HER BACK

1   HMM HMM HMM
2   IF THIS CASE PAYS OFF THEN ON TO THE BIG TIME

1   I SUPPOSE A REENACTMENT OF THE CASE IS NECESSARY
2   YOU KNOW THAT EXPERIENCE IN COURT WOULD MAKE A GOOD MOVIE

1   AND THEY WOULD CALL CLANTON KLUX
2   NEXT . . .

1   I DON'T WANT TO GIVE AWAY THE PLOT—IT'S ABOUT A PLANECRASH AND PILOT—IT LIKE
     TRYING NOT TO RETIRE AND DIE IN BED IN CHINA.
1 & 2   SUPPOSE THERE WAS A PLANECRASH AND EVERYONE DIED BUT THE PILOT.

(WARDEN ENTERS)

WARDEN: HOLD IT. (TO 1 AND 2)
(THE GRID COMES DOWN. 1A AND 2A ENTER AND SIT ON CHAIRS IN FRONT OF GRID)

ACT I
SECTION 4

1A   WHY ARE YOU CRYING
2A   BECAUSE OF THAT TIN CAN

1A   OK OK
2A   HM HM HM

1A   WELL OK OK WHY NOT? WHY NOT?
2A   (IN A VERY LOW VOICE AS IF A RADIO IN THE DISTANCE)
     BORIS CHRISTOPHE PLAY BY TAXES AND COUNCIL YOU READ ABOUT AND FAMILY HELP
     YOU LIVELYHOOD SOMETIMES CONTROVERSIAL 8 O'CLOCK ROMAN NUMBER 3 BUY NEW
     YORK 526 WHAT CAN YOU POSSIBLY NOW THERE ARE WHO HAS TO TAKE CARE OF.

1A   HELLO MIKE
     HELLO MIKE (ECHO)
2A   THIS IS IT—WATCH THE DOOR

1A   AH HUNK
     AH HUNK

2A   (WHISPER SOMETHING BARELY AUDIBLE)   AH HUNK AH HUNK

1A   I'M WALKING RIGHT INTO THE PHONE NEXT TIME
2A   AND THEY SAID "NO"?

1A   ARE YOU FEELING PRETTY GOOD
2A   THEY WALK LIKE THIS

1A   WHAT KIND?
2A   WATCH IT DEAR

1A   OK
2A   OK

1A   YEAH RIGHT
2A   TRY NOT TO OPEN IT TOO FAST

1A & 2A   WHEEL WHAT WHEN NOW HOW
                              OK
              THERE THERE THERE THERE (PAUSE)
              THERE THERE THERE THERE (PAUSE)
                              OK
1A & 2A   YOUR TAPE RECORDER AND TAPES IN THIS BAG

1A   THE SUNDANCE KID WAS BEAUTIFUL

(CHRIS ENTERS)
CHRIS: SPUPS   SPUPS   SPUPS   SPUPS
                      SPUPS   SPUPS   SPUPS   SPUPS
                      SPUPS   SPUPS   SPUPS   SPUPS
                      SPUPS   SPUPS   SPUPS   SPUPS
                      SPUPS   SPUPS   SPUPS   SPUPS
                      SPUPS   SPUPS   SPUPS   SPUPS
                      SPUPS   SPUPS   SPUPS   SPUPS
                      SPUPS   SPUPS   SPUPS   SPUPS
                      SPUPS   SPUPS   SPUPS   SPUPS

2A   I DIDN'T LIKE THE HUMOR

1A   THEN SOMETIMES IT WAS BEAUTIFUL
2A   I DIDN'T THINK SO

1A   THE SUNDANCE KID WAS BEAUTIFUL
2A   AN AWFUL LOT OF FIGHTING IN IT

1A   A LOT OF FIGHTING   LIKE A MOVIE ONE OF THEM LIKE A MOVIE OR SOMETHING
2A   IS HE SHOT? PAUL NEWMAN I MEAN

1A   MAYBE   I DON'T KNOW THOSE WORDS   I CAN'T SAY THEM
        THE SUNDANCE KID IS BEAUTIFUL

AND THE STORY IS ABOUT THE SUNDANCE KID
AND THE MOVIE IS ABOUT THE SUNDANCE KID
AND THE SUNDANCE KID IS BEAUTIFUL
BEAUTIFUL
YEAH THE SUNDANCE KID WAS BEAUTIFUL
YEAH THE SUNDANCE KID IS BEAUTIFUL
YEAH THE SUNDANCE KID IS VERY BEAUTIFUL
YEAH THE SUNDANCE KID CAN
DO THE DANCE
DO THE DANCE A LITTLE BIT
THE SUNDANCE KID COULD DANCE AROUND THE ROOM
THE SUNDANCE KID COULD WALK AROUND THE ROOM
THE SUNDANCE KID COULD RUN AROUND THE ROOM
ABOUT THE HOUSES
HOUSES OF TREES
2A   PLAYGROUNDS
1A   YEAH
YEAH THE SUNDANCE WAS BEAUTIFUL
THE SUNDANCE KID WAS BEAUTIFUL
BECAUSE HE WAS BEAUTIFUL
VERY BEAUTIFUL
THE BEAUTIFUL SUNDANCE KID
THE SUNDANCE KID WAS BEAUTIFUL
THE SUNDANCE KID COULD DANCE AROUND
THE SUNDANCE KID COULD DANCE AROUND THE ROOM
THE SUNDANCE KID WAS BEAUTIFUL BECAUSE
THE SUNDANCE KID COULD DANCE AROUND A LOT
YEAH THE SUNDANCE KID WAS BEAUTIFUL
YEAH
BEAUTIFUL
SO BEAUTIFUL
SO VERY BEAUTIFUL
A LITTLE BIT BEAUTIFUL
A BEAUTIFUL DANCER
A LITTLE BIT BEAUTIFUL
SO THE SUNDANCE KID DID THE DANCING
YEAH THE SUNDANCE KID DOES THE DANCING
SO THE SUNDANCE KID WAS BEAUTIFUL
BECAUSE THE SUNDANCE KID WAS BEAUTIFUL
YEAH THE SUNDANCE KID WAS BEAUTIFUL
WAS BEAUTIFUL
YEAH THE SUNDANCE KID WAS BEAUTIFUL
YEAH THE SUNDANCE KID WAS BEAUTIFUL
IT WAS BEAUTIFUL
THE SUNDANCE KID WAS BEAUTIFUL
YEAH IT WAS BEAUTIFUL
THE
BEAUTIFUL BEAUTIFUL
THE SUNDANCE KID COULD DANCE AROUND
SO THE SUNDANCE KID WAS BEAUTIFUL
YEAH

DANCE DANCED
THE SUNDANCE KID WAS BEAUTIFUL
SO THE HAPPINESS IS THE SUNDANCE KID
THE SUNDANCE KID IS BEAUTIFUL
THE SUNDANCE KID IS BEAUTIFUL
THE SUNDANCE KID WAS BEAUTIFUL
THE SUNDANCE KID DANCED A LOT
DANCE DANCE
DANCED AND DANCING
THROW THE "D" OUT THE WINDOW
AND ADD THE "ING"
THEN RAISE RAISE RAISE YOUR HAND
DANCE DANCING
THE SUNDANCE KID WAS BEAUTIFUL
THE SUNDANCE KID DANCED A LOT
THE SUNDANCE KID DANCED AROUND THE ROOM
RAISING RAISING
RAISE RACE RACING
THE SUNDANCE KID RAISE DANCE RACE
DANCE DANCING
RAISE RAISING
RACE RACING
YEAH THE SUNDANCE KID COULD DANCE A LOT
BUT THE SUNDANCE KID COULD DANCE A LOT
THE SUNDANCE KID COULD DANCE A LOT
YEAH THE SUNDANCE KID COULD DANCE A LOT
YEAH THE SUNDANCE KID WAS VERY BEAUTIFUL
YEAH THE SUNDANCE KID WAS VERY VERY BEAUTIFUL
YEAH THE SUNDANCE KID WAS VERY VERY VERY BEAUTIFUL
YEAH THE SUNDANCE KID WAS VERY VERY VERY VERY VERY VERY BEAUTIFUL
THE SUNDANCE KID DANCES A LOT
THE SUNDANCE KID DANCES VERY VERY VERY WELL
GEORGE ASHLEY HAS A BIG CLOCK
IT TELLS WHAT TIME IT IS
THERE IS A CLOCK
CLOCK CLOCK CLOCK ABOVE
AND IT IS BEAUTIFUL
THE SUNDANCE KID WAS BEAUTIFUL
TO KNOW THAT THE SUNDANCE KID WAS BEAUTIFUL
TO KNOW THE SUNDANCE KID DANCES A LOT
THE SUNDANCE KID WAS BEAUTIFUL
THE SUNDANCE KID WAS VERY VERY VERY VERY BEAUTIFUL
UP IN THE AIR
THE SUNDANCE KID WAS BEAUTIFUL
YEAH BOOM
YEAH THE SUNDANCE KID WAS BEAUTIFUL
YEAH THE SUNDANCE KID WAS LIGHT BROWN BROWN
A KIND OF YELLOW
SOMETHING LIKE THAT
BROWN A KIND OF YELLOW
(CURTAIN)

ENTR'ACTE #1

(CHRIS ON STAGE RIGHT AND BOB ON STAGE LEFT, EACH CLAPPING TWO WOODEN BLOCKS IN
THEIR HANDS. SHOW CURTAIN IS BEHIND THEM.)

```
1   HAP   HATH   HAT   HAP
    HAP   HATH   HAT   HAP
    HAP   HATH   HAT   HAP
    HAP   HATH   HAT   HAP
    HAP   HATH   HAT   HAP
    HAP   HATH   HAT   HAP
    HAP   HATH   HAT   HAP
    HAP   HATH   HAT   HAP
```

2   (AT THE SAME TIME AS 1)

```
    THE   RED   BED   PIECE
    THE   RED   BED   PIECE
    THE   RED   BED   PIECE
    THE   RED   BED   PIECE
    THE   RED   BED   PIECE
    THE   RED   BED   PIECE
    THE   RED   BED   PIECE
    THE   RED   BED   PIECE
```

```
1   THE   RED   BED   PIECE
    THE   RED   BED   PIECE
    THE   RED   BED   PIECE
    THE   RED   BED   PIECE
    THE   RED   BED   PIECE
    THE   RED   BED   PIECE
    THE   RED   BED   PIECE
    THE   RED   BED   PIECE
```

2   (AT THE SAME TIME AS 1)

```
    HAP   HATH   HAP   HAT
    HAP   HATH   HAP   HAT
    HAP   HATH   HAP   HAT
    HAP   HATH   HAP   HAT
    HAP   HATH   HAP   HAT
    HAP   HATH   HAP   HAT
    HAP   HAT    HAP   HATH
    HAP   HATH   HAP   HAT
```

2   COSABI NHJGT BNHG VFCD CVFESW XCVF BGH NMKJI MNHJUYGTHFRD VBNH BG V
    B BBNHJ BGV PER GLOS O CHOCOLATE.
1   WHAT
2   TYUJHYGFR NHJUKIIOOL MNHBG VFG CDXCVFGBHNJUYT BNHGT VFCD H HGJYUU GHU
    GLOS O CHOCOLATE.
1   WHAT

2 GHUJYGTFRDECVBNHGTYH VBGH NHBGV FACHE DFGTYHJK BNHJMKIUHY FACHE SDFG
   CIUHJ. FGHYTFRDEF POULET GHYTF PER GLOS CHOCOLATE.
2 LOOOGGFGHYTGFRBNHGT VFGBNJUYTRFGHJNBVFGH CVFGBHNJ GLOS O CHOCOLATE.
1 SUYTG YHJU BN. VFVBHGFCFRTGHYUJKINBGHYTGFRCDERFGTHYJUNB GHYUJ-
   KIUJHYTGFRDECVFGBNHJMKIUUYGTHJUHGTFRDJK VBGF GHU GLOS O CHOCOLATE.
2 WHAT
1 SOIUYTNCVFGBNHJUYHGTFRDFVBNNHJKKIUJHYGTFDDERRFGHYTGGGHH   VBG-
   HNMJKLPOIUY RRRFGGHJJKMNH ROUGE DFGHNNMJK HNBG ROUGE BNHG ROUGE. SOIU
   UIF YUFRCF YUI GLAOSES. GHYTFGRDE BNHG DE PARIS. SUYHGT TGHT FRANCAIS.
   FGHYTFD SELF SERVICE. DOIU YUI KNHUY JAYE. DFGTRVB MEY FROIND. SOIUJHY BGH
   JHYT TELEPHONE POLICE. SOI GHYUJ POLICE GOIUT FGHET FAHCE FACHE CHGTYH. SOI
   GHOIU POLICE GOIUT FGHT FACHE DFGTHY B. SOI GHUJ POLICE GOIUT FGHY
   FAHCE. DEPOIKJU BNHGTY VBGF PROISOUNB. DFRGT. THRETDFGHYBUJHYG
   BGHNMJKIUHJYGTFRD CVBGFHYUJKI BVGHNMJ BNHJUI VBGHY CVFGBHNJMKIJUH VBG-
   HYUJKIJNBHGVBNHJMKIJUHYGTFRFGT VBGH GHU GLOS O CHOCOLATE.
1 WHAT
   THERE ARE THESE ELECTRO WHE WHE WHE WHE WHE WHE WHE WHE WHE WHEELS
2 THERE ARE THESE AN ELECTRO WHEELS
1 WHAT
2 THERE ARE THESE AN ELECTRO WHE WHE WHE WHE WHE WHE WHE WHEELS
1 THERE ARE THESE ELECTRO WHE WHE WHE WHE WHE WHE WHE WHE WHE WHEELS WHE WHEEL
   WHEELS SO THAT WE CAN HEAR
2 THERE ARE THESE AN ELECTRO WHE WHE WHE WHE WHE WHE WHE WHEEL WHEELS
1 WHAT
2 THERE ARE THESE AN ELECTRO WHEELS SO THAT WE CAN DO THERE ARE THESE AN
   ELECTRO WHEELS
1 WHAT
2 THERE ARE THESE
(1 AND 2 SIMULTANEOUSLY)
1 THERE ARE THESE ELECTRO   WHEWHEWHEWHEWHEWHEE
                               WHEWHEWHEWHEWHEELS
2 THERE ARE THESE AN ELECTRO WHEWHEWHEWHEWHEWHE
                               WHEWHEELS
1 WHAT
2 WE'RE DOING THE FOUR ACTS ACT ONE ACT TWO ACT THREE AND ACT FOUR
1 WHAT
2 WE'RE DOING "A LETTER FOR QUEEN VICTORIA"
1 WHAT
2 WE'RE DOING THE SPEAKING
1 WHAT ARE WE DOING
2 WE'RE DOING THE BLOCKS
1 WHAT ARE WE DOING
2 WE'RE DOING THE PLAY
1 WHAT ARE WE DOING
2 WE JUST DID ACT ONE AND WE'RE GOING TO BE DOING ACT TWO ACT THREE AND ACT
   FOUR
1 WHAT ARE WE DOING
2 YOU DID THE HAP HATHS AND I DID THE RED BED PIECE THEN I DID THE HAP HATHS AND
   YOU DID THE RED BED PIECE THEN WE DID THERE ARE THESE AN ELECTRO WHEELS
1 WHAT ARE WE DOING

```
2   WE'RE
1   WHAT ARE WE DOING
2   WE'RE
1   WHAT    WHAT
    WHAT    WHAT
    WHAT    WHAT
    WHAT    WHAT    ARE   WE
            WHAT    ARE   WE
            WHAT    ARE   WE
            WHAT    ARE   WE
            WHAT    ARE   WE    DOING
2   WE'RE DOING "A LETTER FOR QUEEN VICTORIA"
1   AND YOU SIT ON THE BENCH
2   AND YOU WAIT FOR ME
1   AND YOU SIT ON THE BENCH
2   AND YOU WAIT FOR ME
1   AND YOU SIT ON THE BENCH
2   AND YOU WAIT FOR ME
1   AND YOU SIT ON THE BENCH
2   AND YOU WAIT FOR ME
2   AND YOU SIT ON THE BENCH
1   AND YOU WAIT FOR ME
2   AND YOU SIT ON THE BENCH
1   AND YOU WAIT FOR ME
2   AND YOU SIT ON THE BENCH
1   AND YOU WAIT FOR ME
2   AND YOU SIT ON THE BENCH
1   AND YOU WAIT FOR ME
```

(1 AND 2 SIMULTANEOUSLY)

```
1   AND WAIT FOR ME AND YOU WAIT FOR ME AND YOU WAIT FOR ME
    TILL I COME BACK
2   AND YOU WAIT FOR ME AND WAIT FOR ME AND YOU WAIT FOR
    ME WHEN I COME BACK
1   AND YOU SIT ON THE BENCH AND YOU WAIT FOR ME
    AND YOU WAIT FOR ME TILL I COME BACK
2   AND YOU SIT ON THE BENCH AND YOU WAIT FOR ME
    AND WAIT FOR ME WHEN I COME BACK
1   OK
2   OK
1   OK
2   AOK
1   AO
2   O
1   OK   OK
2   OK
1   OK
2   OK
```

(LIGHTS OUT)

ACT II
SECTION 1A

(CURTAIN UP)

(THERE ARE FOUR PRELIMINARY TABLEAU SCENES. EACH LASTS TWO SECONDS AND IS
FOLLOWED BY A BLACKOUT. A DIFFERENT SLIDE OF AN OSCILLOSCOPE PATTERN IS SHOWN
DURING EACH OF THE FOUR SCENES.)

1   IT DOESN'T SEEM RIGHT
2   I KNOW
3   YEP, WHAT'S HAPPENING
4   JOINING JACK

1   TURNING DOWN THE LIGHTS   GET ON OUT OF HERE
2   RIDE IN THE WHIRLWIND   IT LOOKS CLEAR
3   MAKE YOUR HOUSE BEAUTIFUL
4   OH

1   IT'S A LONG RIDE   WHY DON'T YOU STEP DOWN
2   YOU CAN CALL ME BLIND DICK
3   COME ON
4   NO?

1   WHERE?
2   THERE FIVE OF YOU   DID ANYONE TIE YOU UP AROUND THE TREE
3   WHAT'S WRONG WITH HIM
4   WHY?

1   IF EVER I'VE SEEN ANY
2   (QUICK) HOW ABOUT FELL ON HIS NIGHT?
3   SOMETHING RABBIT
4   MAYBE YOU DO, BURN?

1   IT WILL BE LIGHT NOW TOMORROW
2   ALLA LE ZEEION
3   I DIDN'T MIND IT
4   IN LIKE OF WHAT I'VE GOT?

1   THINK WE OUGHT TO PUT A WATCH ON IT?
2   JUST LIKE US DON'T KNOW
3   MIGHT BE

(3 FALLS)
(CIVIL WAR SOLDIER CROSSES SINGING SILENTLY)
JIM: (SILENTLY) COME IN.

4   DIDN'T SEEM MUCH TO ME

1   ONCE OR TWICE
2   I'VE BEEN DOING IT A WHILE
3   HE'S GOT ONE THERE
4   I KNOW IT AIN'T CRAZY   I'M GOING TO THINK ABOUT IT AS SOON AS I GET OUT OF HERE
     TOMORROW

1   I WAS WONDERING IF IT WAS THE ONE
2   I'M NOT GOING TO GET STARTED EVEN WITH THIS MORNING, BURN
3   YEAH ANYTIME NOW   WHAT DO WE DO THEN?
4   YOU GOT NO CHANCE

1   WE WON'T WAIT FOREVER (YELLED)
2   HELLO (WHISPERED VERY LOUD)
3   THIS IS OUR ONLY CHANCE
4   IT LONG DAY

1   RUNNING BACK AND FORTH
2   AAAH (IN A LOW FAINT VOICE)
3   NOW DON'T TAKE CHANCE
4   HEAVY

                              1
            OK   WELL I GUESS WE COULD   AH...
            OK   WELL I GUESS WE COULD   AH...
                 WELL   OK OK OK WHAT?

                              2
                         OK OK
                 WELL,   OK OK

                              3
                 WELL   OK OK OK WELL
                 WELL   OK OK OK WELL A
                 WELL   AOK OK OK WELL
                 WELL   OK OK OK WELL

                              4
                 OK OK OK OK OKAY
                 OKAYK OK OK O
                 OK OK OK OK O
                 O

1   SAVE TIME
2   YOU HAVE A LONG WAY TO GO
3   MOVE ON OUT
4   LET'S GO

1   IF THE LEAD CAR RUNS INTO TROUBLE
2   HOW ABOUT NOON TOMORROW?
3   YEAH?
4   I TOLD YOU THAT THEY WERE HERE

1   LOOKS LIKE YOU WERE RIGHT
2   THAT'S RIGHT I HAD IT
3   THAT'S RIGHT I'LL CRASH CAR TOMORROW
4   I WAS SCARED I TELL YOU

1   OK
2   (LAUGH)
3   WHAT DID YOU DO?
4   BETTER WAIT

1   WHAT GOES ON HERE? WHERE ARE THE PLANES
2   SEQUACHEE DAM SEQUACHEE DAM
3   AREN'T YOU GOING TO GIVE ME A RIDE
4   GET BACK TO CAMP

                                              (SOUND OF BLAST)

1   WOW!!! (WHISPERED VERY LOUD)
2   I COUNT TEN . . . FAULKNER
3   IT DIDN'T DO NO GOOD
4   THAT'S RIGHT STUPID

1   WELL YOU THINK ON IT
2   WELL MAYBE WE CAN WORK SOMETHING OUT
3   THOUGHT YOU SAID WE'RE GOING TO KILL THEM
4   FRANK LOOKS KINDA PINK DOESN'T HE

1   THEY MAKE RESPIRATIONS
2   TWO THINGS WE HAVE TO KNOW DO AS I SAY
    WE NEED THOSE STILLS TO SURVIVE THIS IS NO GAME
3   YEAH YEAH RECKON SO
4   SHALL WE DUMP THAT STUFF IN THE WATER AND FIND OUT?

1   I THOUGHT YOU WERE NEVER COMING BACK
2   THEY SAID HE WOULD LIE TO GET WHAT HE WANTS
3   WHAT DO WE HAVE HERE?   HM.

(WARDEN RUNS ONSTAGE)
WARDEN: HOLD IT.

(LIGHTS OUT)

ACT II
SECTION 1B1

(THERE ARE FOUR PRELIMINARY TABLEAU SCENES)

1   IT DOESN'T SEEM RIGHT
2   I KNOW

3   YEP, WHAT'S HAPPENING
4   JOINING JACK

(SOUND OF TRAIN WHISTLE)

1   TURNING DOWN THE LIGHTS   GET ON OUT OF HERE
2   RIDE IN THE WHIRLWIND
    IT LOOKS CLEAR
3   MAKE YOUR HOUSE BEAUTIFUL
4   OH

(SOUND OF HORSES' HOOFS
FOR 20 SECONDS)

1   IT'S A LONG RIDE.   WHY DON'T YOU STEP DOWN
2   YOU CAN CALL ME BLIND DICK
3   COME ON
4   NO?

1   WHERE?
2   THERE 5 OF YOU   DID ANYONE TIE YOU UP AROUND THE TREE
3   WHAT'S WRONG WITH HIM?
4   WHY?

1   IF EVER I'VE SEEN ANY
2   (QUICK) HOW ABOUT FELL ON HIS NIGHT?
3   SOMETHING RABBIT
4   MAYBE YOU DO, BURN?

1   IT WILL BE LIGHT NOW TOMORROW
2   ALLA LE ZEEION
3   I DIDN'T MIND IT

1   THINK WE OUGHT TO PUT A WATCH ON IT?
2   JUST LIKE US DON'T KNOW
3   MIGHT BE
4   DIDN'T SEEM MUCH TO ME

1   ONCE OR TWICE
2   I'VE BEEN DOING IT A WHILE
3   HE'S GOT ONE THERE
4   I KNOW IT AIN'T CRAZY   I'M GOING TO THINK ABOUT IT AS SOON AS I GET OUT OF HERE
    TOMORROW

1   I WAS WONDERING IF IT WAS THE ONE
2   I'M NOT GOING TO GET STARTED EVEN WITH THIS MORNING, BURN.
3   YEAH ANYTIME NOW
    WHAT DO WE DO THEN?   (SOUND OF GUNS FIRING)
4   YOU GOT NO CHANCE

1   (LONG PAUSE) WE WON'T WAIT FOREVER (YELLED)
2   HELLO (WHISPERED VERY LOUD)
3   THIS IS OUR ONLY CHANCE
4   IT LONG DAY

1   RUNNING BACK AND FORTH   (ONE GUN SHOT)

(2 FALLS)

2   AAAAH (IN A LOW FAINT VOICE)
3   NOW DON'T TAKE CHANCE

(2 GETS UP SLOWLY)

4   HEAVY

                          1
            OK   WELL I GUESS WE COULD   AH...
                     (30 SECONDS)
            OK   WELL I GUESS WE COULD   AH...
                     (18 SECONDS)
                WELL   OK OK OK WHAT?

                          2
                     OK OK
                WELL,   OK OK

                          3
                WELL   OK OK OK WELL
                WELL   OK OK OK WELL A
                WELL AOK OK OK WELL
                WELL   OK OK OK WELL

                          4
                OK OK OK OK OKAY
                OKAYK OK OK O
                OK OK OK OK O
                O

1   SAVE TIME

(CHRIS ENTERS AND MAKES TAPERCORDING)
                          CHRIS
            PIRUP   BIRUP   PIRUP   BIRUP
            PIRUP   BIRUP   PIRUP   BIRUP
            PIRUP   BIRUP   PIRUP   BIRUP
            PIRUP   BIRUP   PIRUP   BIRUP
            PIRUP   BIRUP   PIRUP   BIRUP
            PIRUP   BIRUP   PIRUP   BIRUP
            PIRUP   BIRUP   PIRUP   BIRUP
            PIRUP   BIRUP   PIRUP   BIRUP
            PIRUP   BIRUP   PIRUP   BIRUP

2   YOU HAVE A LONG WAY TO GO
3   MOVE ON OUT
4   LET'S GO

1   IF THE LEAD CAR RUNS INTO TROUBLE
2   HOW ABOUT NOON TOMORROW?
3   YEAH?
4   I TOLD YOU THAT THEY WERE HERE

1   LOOKS LIKE YOU WERE RIGHT
2   THAT'S RIGHT I HAD IT
3   THAT'S RIGHT I'LL CRASH CAR TOMORROW
4   I WAS SCARED I TELL YOU

1   OK
2   (LAUGH)
3   WHAT DID YOU DO?
4   BETTER WAIT

1   WHAT GOES ON HERE? WHERE ARE THE PLANES?
2   SEQUATCHEE DAM SEQUATCHEE DAM
3   AREN'T YOU GOING TO GIVE ME A RIDE?
4   GET BACK TO CAMP

                                              (SOUND OF BLAST)
1   WOW!!! (WHISPERED VERY LOUD)
2   I COUNT TEN . . . FAULKNER
3   IT DIDN'T DO NO GOOD
4   THAT'S RIGHT STUPID

1   WELL YOU THINK ON IT
2   WELL MAYBE WE CAN WORK SOMETHING OUT
3   THOUGHT YOU SAID WE'RE GOING TO KILL THEM
4   FRANK LOOKS KINDA PINK DOESN'T HE

1   THEY MAKE RESPIRATIONS
2   TWO THINGS WE HAVE TO KNOW DO AS I SAY
    WE NEED THOSE STILLS TO SURVIVE THIS IS NO GAME

3   YEAH YEAH RECKON SO
4   SHALL WE DUMP THAT STUFF IN THE WATER AND FIND OUT

1   I THOUGHT YOU WERE NEVER COMING BACK
2   THEY SAID HE WOULD LIE TO GET WHAT HE WANTS
3   WHAT DO WE HAVE HERE?   HMMM.

(WARDEN RUNS ONSTAGE)

WARDEN: HOLD IT.

(LIGHTS OUT)

ACT II
SECTION 2

(LIGHTS UP)

(EVERYONE LYING ON FLOOR BUT 2)

2   CLANTON KLUX
     YEAH
     THE STILL
     YEAH I GOT YOU
     UM HM UM HM UM HM UM HM
     EXACTLY LIKE THAT
     SOMETHING LIKE THAT

(LIGHTS OUT, EVERYONE STANDS, LIGHTS UP)

(CIVIL WAR SOLDIER ENTERS SINGING)

C.W.S.: WE DON'T TAKE MAKE MUCH FOR WHITE BOY'S WORK.

(CIVIL WAR SOLDIER EXITS)
(2 COPIES ALL ACTIONS OF CIVIL WAR SOLDIER, MOUTHS WORDS, SINGS SONG VERY LOUD)

2   HEY SHE'S BEEN AROUND HERE FOR YEARS.
3   YOU WILL SEE THAT STILL IN DUE TIME
4   WE MANAGE

1   HONEY DON'T TIE YOURSELF ON THE DISHES

(2 AND 3 HAVE FIGHT, ALTERNATING HMM'S AND POUND EACH OTHER'S SHOULDERS)

3   WELL OK
2   WE KILLED YOUR BROTHER AND WE FEEL REAL BAD ABOUT IT
3   LET'S GO ON DOWN AND SEE
4   WELL IT LOOKS LIKE YOUR BOYS HAVE DONE THEIR JOB PARTNER

1   TELL THEM WE HEARD FROM JIM
2   I'M SURPRISED YOU KNOW TO LET LAW HANDLE THESE MATTERS

3   WHAT MAN WILL GUESS
4   WHAT NEXT WILL YOU DO

1   NO NO I'LL STOP THEM
2   I'M NEED YOUR HELP   YOU'RE THE ONLY ONE THAT KNOWS
3   WELL IT'S NOT THAT . . . IT'S JUST THAT I DON'T WANT TO GET LONELY
4   ARE YOU SERIOUS, COME ON LET'S GO

1   NOT TODAY
2   COME ON GET OUT UP HERE

3   WELL IF THERE'RE NOT BACK IN AN HOUR
4   I SAW THE STILLS (WHISPERED)

1   I SAW THE WHOLE THING
2   THEY COVERED THE WHOLE PLACE WITH IT   IT'S JUST MIXING ALL MUD
3   THEY'RE GOING TO HAVE TO SEND DOWN SIX MORE
4   YEAHA

1   THEY KNOW WHO YOU ARE
2   THEN THEY ARE GOING ON TO THE STILL
3   YOU ARE ON YOUR OWN
4   LOOKS LIKE WE . . . I'M NOT FRANK

1   PUT HIM ON THE PAD
2   I CARRIED MICROPHONE, TYPE RECORDERS
3   WHO IS GOING TO COME FORTH AND TESTIFY
4   NO I WON'T ASK YOU THAT

1   I KNOW WHAT I WAS DOING   I WOULDN'T DO THAT AGAIN—I MADE MY BED I'VE GOT TO
    LIE IN IT
2   I REALLY WORRY ABOUT THAT
3   JUSTICE SHOULD BE HEARD EQUALLY   LA JUSTICE DEVRAIT ÊTRE ENTENDU ÉGALEMENT.
2   (SCREAM/SONG)

(LIGHTS OUT)

ACT II
SECTION 1B2

(THERE ARE THREE PRELIMINARY TABLEAU SCENES. EACH LASTS TWO SECONDS AND IS
FOLLOWED BY A BLACKOUT.)

1   IT DOESN'T SEEM RIGHT
2   I KNOW
3   YEP, WHAT'S HAPPENING
4   JOINING JACK
                                                    (SOUND OF TRAIN WHISTLE)
1   TURNING DOWN THE LIGHTS GET ON OUT OF HERE
2   RIDE IN THE WHIRLWIND IT LOOKS CLEAR   (SOUNDS OF HORSES' HOOFS
3   MAKE YOUR HOUSE BEAUTIFUL   FOR 20 SECONDS)
4   OH

1   IT'S A LONG RIDE. WHY DON'T YOU STEP DOWN
2   YOU CAN CALL ME BLIND DICK
3   COME ON
4   NO?

1   WHERE?
2   THERE ARE FIVE OF YOU   DID ANYONE TIE YOU UP AROUND THE TREE

3   WHAT'S WRONG WITH HIM?
4   WHY?

1   IF EVER I'VE SEEN ANY
2   (QUICK) HOW ABOUT FELL ON HIS NIGHT
3   SOMETHING RABBIT
4   MAYBE YOU DO, BURN?

1   IT WILL BE LIGHT NOW TOMORROW
2   ALLA LE ZEEION
3   I DIDN'T MIND IT
4   IN LIKE OF WHAT I GOT?

1   THINK WE OUGHT TO PUT A WATCH ON IT?
2   JUST LIKE US DON'T KNOW
3   MIGHT BE
4   DIDN'T SEEM MUCH TO ME

1   ONCE OR TWICE
2   I'VE BEEN DOING IT A WHILE
3   HE'S GOT ONE THERE
4   I KNOW IT AIN'T CRAZY   I'M GOING TO THINK ABOUT IT AS SOON AS I GET OUT OF HERE
    TOMORROW

1   I WAS WONDERING IF IT WAS THE ONE
2   I'M NOT GOING TO GET STARTED EVEN WITH THIS MORNING, BURN.
3   YEAH ANYTIME NOW
    WHAT DO WE DO THEN?   (SOUND OF GUNS FIRING)
4   YOU GOT NO CHANCE

1   (LONG PAUSE) WE WON'T WAIT FOREVER (YELLED)
2   HELLO (WHISPERED VERY LOUD)
3   THIS IS OUR ONLY CHANCE   (LOTS OF GUN FIRE)
4   IT LONG DAY

1   RUNNING BACK AND FORTH
                                                         (ONE GUN SHOT)

(2 FALLS)

2   AAAAH (IN A LOW FAINT VOICE)
3   NOW DON'T TAKE CHANCE

(2 GETS UP SLOWLY)

4   HEAVY

                              1
              OK   WELL I GUESS WE COULD   AH...
                        (15 SECONDS)
              OK   WELL I GUESS WE COULD   AH...
                        (10 SECONDS)
                  WELL   OK OK OK WHAT?

```
                    2
               OK OK
       WELL,   OK OK


                    3
       WELL    OK OK OK WELL
       WELL    OK OK OK WELL A
       WELL  AOK OK OK WELL
       WELL    OK OK OK WELL


                    4
        OK  OK  OK OK OKAY
        OKAYK  OK OK O
        OK  OK  OK OK O
        O
```

1   SAVE TIME

(CHRIS ENTERS AND MAKES TAPERECORDING)

```
                    CHRIS
       PIRUP   BIRUP   PIRUP   BIRUP
       PIRUP   BIRUP   PIRUP   BIRUP
       PIRUP   BIRUP   PIRUP   BIRUP
       PIRUP   BIRUP   PIRUP   BIRUP
       PIRUP   BIRUP   PIRUP   BIRUP
       PIRUP   BIRUP   PIRUP   BIRUP
       PIRUP   BIRUP   PIRUP   BIRUP
       PIRUP   BIRUP   PIRUP   BIRUP
       PIRUP   BIRUP   PIRUP   BIRUP
```

2   YOU HAVE A LONG WAY TO GO
3   MOVE ON OUT
4   LET'S GO

1   IF THE LEAD CAR RUNS INTO TROUBLE
2   HOW ABOUT NOON TOMORROW?
3   YEAH?
4   I TOLD YOU THAT THEY WERE HERE

1   LOOKS LIKE YOU WERE RIGHT
2   THAT'S RIGHT I HAD IT
3   THAT'S RIGHT I'LL CRASH CAR TOMORROW
4   I WAS SCARED I TELL YOU

1   OK
2   (LAUGH)
3   WHAT DID YOU DO?
4   BETTER WAIT

1   WHAT GOES ON HERE?   WHERE ARE THE PLANES

2   SEQUACHEE DAM SEQUACHEE DAM
3   AREN'T YOU GOING TO GIVE ME A RIDE
4   GET BACK TO CAMP

                                                        (SOUND OF BLAST)

1   WOW!!! (WHISPERED VERY LOUD)
2   I COUNT TEN . . . FAULKNER
3   IT DIDN'T DO NO GOOD
4   THAT'S RIGHT STUPID

1   WELL YOU THINK ON IT
2   WELL MAYBE WE CAN WORK SOMETHING OUT
3   THOUGHT YOU SAID WE'RE GOING TO KILL THEM
4   FRANK LOOKS KINDA PINK DOESN'T HE

1   THEY MAKE RESPIRATIONS
2   TWO THINGS WE HAVE TO KNOW DO AS I SAY
    WE NEED THOSE STILLS TO SURVIVE   THIS IS NO GAME

3   YEAH YEAH RECKON SO
4   SHALL WE DUMP THAT STUFF IN THE WATER AND FIND OUT?

1   I THOUGHT YOU WERE NEVER COMING BACK
2   THEY SAID HE WOULD LIE TO GET WHAT HE WANTS
3   WHAT DO WE HAVE HERE?   HMMM.

(WARDEN RUNS ONSTAGE)

WARDEN: HOLD IT.

(LIGHTS OUT)

ACT II
SECTION 3

(LIGHTS UP)

1   I UNDERSTAND YOU WERE A SLAVE
2   WELL THERE WERE LOTS OF SLAVES
3   I'LL PROVE IT TO YOU
4   LOTS OF LUCK

1   THIS IS THE INCREASING VALUE
2   GOOD EVENING   THANK YOU FOR BEING HERE (WHISPERED VERY LOUD)
3   WE HAVE NO CONTROL OVER HIS ACTION   PIRUP PIRUP PIRUP PIRUP PIRUP PIRUP
    (PIRUPS SUNG)
4   THIS IS THE RABBIT

1   THERE IS NO ASSERTION OF MULTIPLE POWER
2   IS THAT THERE THE SUBPOENA THAT REQUIRES HIS APPEARANCE

3   THERE ARE NO BASIS THAT HE HAS BEEN LYING
4   HE'S EVEN MORE PESSIMISTIC ABOUT AN END TO THE RECEPTION

1   IT'S CAUSING A LOT OF HARDSHIPS
2   YOU PAY AND PAY AND PAY AND PAY
3   HE'S CREDIT RATING IS GOING
4   SEEN FROM HIS OWN PERSONAL VIEW WHY SHOULD HE?

1   YOU'RE IN LUCK WHEN YOU SEE WHAT MANDA SAW
2   THERE IS NO CONNECTION   EACH WALKED AND STOOD ALONE   PIRUP
3   IT'S NOT GOING TO PUT YOU OFF THE STREET
4   THE CHINESE FORCES TOOK THE PARASEL ISLAND

(CIVIL WAR SOLDIER ENTERS PULLING MANY BOXES, WHILE WALKING, SINGS THE FOLLOW-
ING ARIA)

C.W.S.   IT'S SEVEN O'CLOCK AND THE GENERAL'S NOT HERE YET
         HE MUST BE HAVING HIS SUPPER OR TARDY

         HE SAID HE'D MEET ME
         IN FRONT OF THE DRUGSTORE
         I BELIEVED HIM
         SO NOW I'M WAITING
         IMPATIENTLY FOR HIM TO COME
         I THOUGHT I HEARD
         SOMEONE KNOCKING AT THE DOOR!
         IT'S GETTING LATER AND
         LATER AND LATER
         HE'D BETTER COME PRETTY SOON
         OR I'LL SCREAM

                                                              (2 SCREAMS)

         AH!
         I WONDER WHAT EVER COULD BE KEEPING HIM?
         IT'S NOT AT ALL WHAT I'D EXPECT OF HIM
         WHO DOES HE THINK HE IS?

         I THINK I'LL JUST CALL MY LAWYER UP
         RIGHT AWAY
         BEFORE I TAKE A NAP ON THE SOFA HERE

                                                     (KNOCK KNOCK KNOCK)

         WHO'S THERE?

JIM: COME IN.

(JIM AND CIVIL WAR SOLDIER EXIT)

1   IT'S A LIFE SAVER FOR BUSY PEOPLE
2   AND FINALLY TONIGHT
3   THIS ATOM BOMB IS IMPOSSIBLE   BIRUP
4   YEAH THIS LITTLE FELLOW WILL BE GRAND CHAMPION

1   BUMBLE
2   WHAT I'M DOING HERE IS DEVELOPING A PICTURE
3   WHAT YOU DO IS PRESS THIS OVER HERE
4   NOW I'M FIXING TO DEVELOP

1   HELLO I'M WALLY LOW LOW
2   HELLO HOW ARE YOU
3   SUPPOSE WE COULD SPEED IT UP THE
4   WAY WE DO I WATCH

1   THEN I SUPPOSE WE COULD
2   FIGURE SOMETHING OUT
3   WHY SIR THAT PERFECTLY ALL RIGHT
4   THANK YOU

1   THE STANDARD TIME LOCK NO PROBLEM
2   YOU WILL HAVE TO REMOVE THE CORD—THAT'S ALL WE NEED
3   CAN I COLLECTIVELY ASSUME WE HAVE AN AGREEMENT
4   BUT THERE ARE MORE COMING IN

1   YOU BETTER GET ON TO THEM
2   RIGHT
3   AND WHAT WOULD YOU LIKE ME TO DO?
                                                    (SOUND OF DOOR KNOCKING)
4   LET ME WIN

1   RIGHT?
2   SOMETHING LIKE THAT
3   YOU PUT ONE OF MY MEN DOWN THERE
4   WHAT WAS THAT

1   FABULOUS
2   RELIVE THOSE FABULOUS MOMENTS
3   SUSSEX COUNTY
    SUSFUIL COUNTY
    ESSEX COUNT
            COUNTY
    OK LET'S GO   (LAUGH)

4   AH UN   AH UN   AH UN   AH UN
                AH UN   AH UN   AH UN   AH UN
                AH UN   AH UN   AH UN   AH UN

1   AH UN   AH UN   AH UN   AH UN
                AH UN   AH UN   AH UN   AH UN
                AH UN   AH UN   AH UN   AH UN

2   CONGRATULATIONS
3   CONGRATULATIONS
4   CONGRATULATIONS

(2 FALLS)

3   SOMEONE CALL A DOCTOR PEOPLE WILL BE HERE VERY SOON
4   WHAT IS IT?

1   WHERE IS THE CITY HEALTH DEPARTMENT
2   IS THAT THE LAST OF THEM

3

THANK YOU	THANK YOU	THANK YOU	THANK YOU
THANK YOU	THANK YOU	THANK YOU	THANK YOU
THANK YOU	THANK YOU	THANK YOU	THANK YOU
THANK YOU	THANK YOU	THANK YOU	THANK YOU
THANK YOU	THANK YOU	THANK YOU	THANK YOU
THANK YOU	THANK YOU	THANK YOU	THANK YOU

(CIVIL WAR SOLDIER ENTERS, LOOKS AT 2, SOUND OF EXPLOSION AND CLOCKS TICKING VERY FAST, CIVIL WAR SOLDIER EXITS)

1
HOW MUCH FASTER

THANK YOU	THANK YOU	THANK YOU	THANK YOU
THANK YOU	THANK YOU	THANK YOU	THANK YOU
THANK YOU	THANK YOU	THANK YOU	THANK YOU
THANK YOU	THANK YOU	THANK YOU	THANK YOU
THANK YOU	THANK YOU	THANK YOU	THANK YOU
THANK YOU	THANK YOU	THANK YOU	THANK YOU

4

THANK YOU	THANK YOU	THANK YOU	THANK YOU
THANK YOU	THANK YOU	THANK YOU	THANK YOU
THANK YOU	THANK YOU	THANK YOU	THANK YOU
THANK YOU	THANK YOU	THANK YOU	THANK YOU
THANK YOU	THANK YOU	THANK YOU	THANK YOU
THANK YOU	THANK YOU	THANK YOU	THANK YOU

2
TO WITHSTAND EARTHQUAKES

(3 OPENS 1 BOX, REMOVES METAL CONTAINER, HOLDS IT OVER 2)

(LONG PAUSE)

3   OK WE HAVE TO GO TO THE UNDERGROUND
4   I KNOW I KNOW IT TAKES A LOT

(A SERIES OF SLIDES OF OSCILLOSCOPE PATTERNS ARE SHOWN, AND THERE IS A TAPERCORD-ING OF NUMBERS)

(LIGHTS OUT)

ACT II
SECTION 4

(LIGHTS UP)

(ALL CRAWL ON FLOOR)

1   IT'S BETTER. DETAILS AT TEN.
2   GOOD LUCK ANYHOW
3   OK, LET'S SEE HOW IT WORKS
4   A RED GIANT IT HAS HAPPENED ELSEWHERE IT HAS NO PATTERN EXCEPT FROM SPRING

1   WE MAY NEVER KNOW WHAT TOOK PLACE HERE   A ONCE GREAT CITY
2   IT WAS REALLY THAT TOOK AWAY THAT CITY
3   OR THESE DESIGNS OF MAN OR EXPERIMENTAL DESIGNS FOR MAN
4   THE SUN GOD OF TEEWEENEAKO WEEPS

1   THE GREAT SNOME OF SIGH WEE
2   MAKING FARMING POSSIBLE EVEN IN THE MOUNTAINS
3   35 HUNDRED FEET UNDER WATER A WALL BERMUDA WALL
4   THE CASE OF THE MISSING PLANES

1   THEY LOOK LIKE THEY ARE AFTER ME   DON'T COME AFTER ME
2   THE PRINCIPLE BASIS FOR LIFE IS PROTEIN

OFFSTAGE VOICE: PROTEINS ARE PRESENT IN EVERY PLANT AND ANIMAL CELL. THEY ARE
POLYMERS BUILT OF AMINO ACIDS, DIFFERENTIATED BY THE ORDER OF THESE ACIDS. THEY
BOND INTO LONG THIN STRANDS USUALLY TIGHTLY WOUND IN THE CELL BUT IN CERTAIN
CELLS, SUCH AS HAIR AND FUR, THEY ARE STRETCHED OUT.

(CHRISTOPHER FLIES ACROSS STAGE)

3   IT MUST HAVE OCCURED MANY TIMES MANY PLACES
4   MAYBE IT WAS DELIBERATELY SENT
3   OK

1   WE COULD UNDERSTAND VERY EASILY
2   THEY SUDDENLY DISAPPEAR AND THEY WERE SO DIFFERENT
3   FROM THE AIR THEY TAKE ON DIFFERENT SHAPES
4   HOW DOES IT WORK   WHAT DOES IT LOOK LIKE

1   A STONE CIRCLE
2   THE HITCHING POST
3   WITH REFERENCE TO TELEVISION
4   IT'S STILL THE PRODUCTION OF RESEARCH

1   TO TRAVEL IN THE SKY
2   A REEL AIRREAL CAR
3   BECAUSE OF THE CIDLY
4   WHAT IS CIDLY

1   HOW DO WE COUNT FOR THE DRAWING
2   A DELTA WING FIGHTER PLANE
3   LINKS THE JUNGLE WITH THE SEA
4   ENORMOUS PINK SCABS O CIDLEY

1   THE ORIGINAL WALLS ARE STANDING
2   NO ONE CAN READ THEM
3   COLORED THREADS
4   THE HOLE OF THE HEAD IS POINT ONE NINE CENTIMETERS

1   RUST FREE IRON PROOF
2   RADIO WAVES CONTROLLING HER BEHAVIOR
3   YEAH YEAH
4   HE SEES FOUR OF THEM

1   SOME HELICOPTERS HAVE THE DISTINCT CONFIGURATION OF FACES
2   GREAT WALLS
3   YEAH CAME TUMBLING DOWN   PLAN YOU WISE
2   THEY PLANTED SUITABLE TREES
3   THE ENTIRE AREA WAS DENSELY CROWDED
4   GARDEN IN THE PLACE OF EXERCISE

1   GET THEE IN HASTE
2   WHAT?
3   15,000 B.C. (LOW VOICE):   (SOUND OF EXPLOSION)
    THERA SARANEA KNEE
4   COULD THERE CONSTRUCTION HE
                                HE

1   WHAT?
2   MYTH MATH MATTER   A RED GIANT   IT HAS HAPPENED ELSEWHERE
3   A SILENT CITY
4   MUD WALLS

1   A STONE GOD
2   IN IMPRINTS
3   SOMETHING WAS ALWAYS MISSING
4   WHEN WE WERE ALL ALONE

1   REACH OUT
2   IS SOMEONE IN SPACE
3   WE WANT TO HELP BILLY
4   WE'RE ALREADY INCOMPETENT

1   ARE WE MAKE UP IT OR NOT
2   SEEMS WE LIVE A DOUBLE LIFE (LOW PITCH AND VOLUME OF VOICE)
3   I CAN'T BELIEVE I COULD
4   I PUT OUT AN A.P.B.

1   ANYTHING ELSE WE WANT TO SAY
2   I DON'T UNDERSTAND IT?

3   BUT WHY DID YOU RUN
4   WHAT CAN I DO FOR YOU

1   THAT WHY WE COME HERE
2   OK WELCOME
3   THANK YOU
4   EVERY ONCE IN A WHILE WE GET SOME FREAKS FROM CHINATOWN

1   HOW COME YOU DON'T HAVE . . .
2   YOU'RE THE ONE WITH A GREAT EAR FOR DETAIL
3   YOU LOOK LIKE A NICE COUPLE

(LIGHTS OUT)

(CURTAIN)
(DARK BREAK DROP OF DAM)

(SCREAM SONG BY ROBERT WILSON.)

ACT III

(LARGE BACKDROP ACROSS STAGE IS PAINTED WITH A SYMMETRICAL DESIGN OF THE WORDS
"CHITTER" "CHATTER.")
ALL: CHITTER   CHATTER   CHITTER   CHATTER
                CHITTER   CHATTER   CHITTER   CHATTER
                CHITTER   CHATTER   CHITTER   CHATTER
                CHITTER   CHATTER   CHITTER   CHATTER
                CHITTER   CHATTER   CHITTER   CHATTER
                CHITTER   CHATTER   CHITTER   CHATTER
                CHITTER   CHATTER   CHITTER   CHATTER
                CHITTER   CHATTER   CHITTER   CHATTER
                CHITTER   CHATTER   CHITTER   CHATTER
                CHITTER   CHATTER   CHITTER   CHATTER

1A   I CANNOT TOLERATE LIVING IN THE CITY ALL YEAR
2A   IF IT WEREN'T FOR OUR COUNTRY HOME I DON'T KNOW WHAT I'D DO

1A   IT'S SUCH A CHARMING PLACE
2A   SO QUAINT YOU KNOW

1A   LET'S AGREE
2A   OH YES LET'S DO

1A   HOW VERY TOUCHING
2A   HOW MOVING

1A   IF ONE COULD ONLY HEAR
2A   FOR EVERY TEAR

1A   HOW VERY QUEER
2A   MY DEAR

1A   IN LOVE
2A   WE BE

                                                            (ONE GUN SHOT)
(2A FALLS OVER)

1B   THE VERY BEST OF LUCK TO YOU IN SELLING IT—WHY A HORSE LIKE THAT SHOULD BE
      BOUGHT IN NO TIME.
2B   I SUPPOSE YOU'RE RIGHT—IN CASES AS EXTREME AS THESE YOUR ADVICE HAS ALWAYS
      BEEN SO HELPFUL.

1B   IT'S THE WEIGHT OF THE MATTER THAT OPPRESSES ME SO
2B   OH DEAR I FORGOT MY GLASSES—WHAT AN ABSOLUTELY STUPID THING TO DO.

1B   I'M TERRIBLY SORRY—DO YOU REMEMBER WHERE YOU WORE THEM LAST
2B   NO, IT'S SLIPPED MY MIND ENTIRELY

1B   DON'T WORRY WE'LL TAKE CARE OF IT
2B   IN DUE TIME, AS IT WERE

1B   HOW INTRIGUING, MY DEAR HENRIETTA
2B   GIVEN ALL THE FACTS ARE SO UNLIKELY

1B   IT COULD BE SO
2B   AND SO IT IS

1B   SO TRUE, MY DEAR
2B   SO VERY TRUE

ALL: OOOOOO

(LONG PAUSE)   (MANY MANY GUN SHOTS)
(SLIDE OF AIRPLANE MOVES STAGE LEFT TO STAGE RIGHT)

1C   IT'S SUCH A PITY SUCH A PITY ISN'T IT
2C   YES ISN'T IT A SHAME

1C   SUCH A SHAME
2C   I AGREE   WHY I WAS JUST SAYING TO MYSELF

1C   THE OTHER DAY
2C   IT'S SO IT'S SO

1C   INEVITABLE
2C   UNAVOIDABLE

1C   IT'S SUCH A PITY
2C   SUCH A SHAME

1C OH YES AND THANK YOU SO MUCH FOR JOINING ME HERE TODAY
2C OH YOU DON'T KNOW WHAT A PLEASURE THIS HAS BEEN FOR ME

                                                        (ONE GUN SHOT)
(2C FALLS OVER)

1D YOU SEE IT'S SO VERY VARIOUSLY ASSEMBLED
2D PRECISELY

1D YES YES YOU COULD LOOK AT IT THAT WAY
2D AND THEN AGAIN THERE'S ALWAYS ANOTHER WAY TO SEE IT

1D YES YES YOU'RE QUITE RIGHT
2D YES YES THERE'S SO VERY VERY MUCH TO BE DONE STILL, ISN'T THERE WHY IS IT SO
    DIFFICULT, TELL ME, WHY IS IT SO VERY DIFFICULT SOMETIMES?

1D (COUGHS) OH EXCUSE ME
2D THAT'S QUITE ALL RIGHT

1D JUST IMAGINE
2D THE WAY WE USUALLY DO

1D NO I DON'T THINK SO   IT DOESN'T SEEM THAT WAY TO ME
2D NO NOT AT ALL, IT'S JUST AS YOU WERE SAYING
                                                        (ONE GUN SHOT)
(1D AND 2D FALL OVER)

1E DID YOU HEAR THAT EVELYN IS GETTING A DIVORCE?
2E OH REALLY—HOW DREADFUL

1E YES I DO BELIEVE IT'S IN THE PAPERS
2E IN THE PAPERS!

1E YES
2E HOW DREADFUL

1E DO YOU SEE A CLOUD
2E YES I DO—OH GRACIOUS YOU'RE RIGHT   THERE IS A CLOUD THERE   ISN'T THERE

1E I DO HOPE IT DOESN'T START RAINING
2E OH THAT WOULD BE SIMPLY TERRIBLE

1E WE REALLY SHOULD SEE MORE OF EACH OTHER DON'T YOU THINK
2E YES THAT'S TRUE   IT'S SUCH A PITY THAT WE DON'T

ALL: OOOOO   OOHHH   AAHHH

(CURTAIN DOWN)

(QUEEN VICTORIA ENTERS STAGE LEFT, STOPS IN PROFILE IN FRONT OF COUPLE 1A AND 2A,
AND SCREAMS THREE TIMES.)

ENTR'ACTE #2

(SHOW CURTAIN DOWN. CHRIS SPINS ON STAGE LEFT DANCER'S PLATFORM TO TAPE OF HIMSELF.)   (INTERMISSION)

TAPE: AND YOU SIT ON THE BENCH AND YOU WAIT FOR ME
AND YOU SIT ON THE BENCH AND YOU WAIT FOR ME
AND YOU SIT ON THE BENCH AND YOU WAIT FOR ME
AND YOU SIT ON THE BENCH AND YOU WAIT FOR ME
AND YOU SIT ON THE BENCH AND YOU WAIT FOR ME
AND YOU SIT ON THE BENCH AND YOU WAIT FOR ME
AND YOU SIT ON THE BENCH AND YOU WAIT FOR ME
AND YOU SIT ON THE BENCH AND YOU WAIT FOR ME
AND YOU SIT ON THE BENCH AND YOU WAIT FOR ME
AND YOU SIT ON THE BENCH AND YOU WAIT FOR ME

AND YOU WAIT FOR ME WHEN I COME BACK

CHRIS: LADIES AND GENTLEMEN
THE FOURTH ACT WILL BEGIN IN TEN MORE MINUTES
LADIES AND GENTLEMEN
THE FOURTH ACT WILL BEGIN IN NINE MORE MINUTES
LADIES AND GENTLEMEN
THE FOURTH ACT WILL BEGIN IN EIGHT MORE MINUTES
LADIES AND GENTLEMEN
THE FOURTH ACT WILL BEGIN IN SEVEN MORE MINUTES
LADIES AND GENTLEMEN
THE FOURTH ACT WILL BEGIN IN SIX MORE MINUTES
LADIES AND GENTLEMEN
THE FOURTH ACT WILL BEGIN IN FIVE MORE MINUTES
LADIES AND GENTLEMEN
THE FOURTH ACT WILL BEGIN IN FOUR MORE MINUTES
LADIES AND GENTLEMEN
THE FOURTH ACT WILL BEGIN IN THREE MORE MINUTES
LADIES AND GENTLEMEN
THE FOURTH ACT WILL BEGIN IN TWO MORE MINUTES
LADIES AND GENTLEMEN
THE FOURTH ACT WILL BEGIN IN TWENTY SECONDS
HAVE A GOOD TIME
LADIES AND GENTLEMEN

(LIGHTS OUT)

ACT IV
SECTION 1

(CURTAIN UP)

4   (CHINAMAN) SO, YOU HAVE SEEN FIT TO ENGAGE ME AGAIN. GOOD. I WOULD NOT BE
BEING ABSOLUTELY FRANK IF I DID NOT ADMIT TO A CERTAIN AMOUNT OF PERSONAL

INTEREST IN THIS CASE AFTER ALL . . . AFTER ALL THESE YEARS. PERSONAL INTEREST
NOT WITHOUT SOME DEGREE OF ADMIRATION FOR—SHALL WE SAY—THE "OTHER SIDE".
WHAT HAS ALWAYS BEEN MOST DIFFICULT IN OUR ENCOUNTERS HAS BEEN THE PERCEP-
TION OF THE SCOPE THE MANEUVERINGS ENCOMPASS. YOU HAVE A TERM—"THE LONG
VIEW"—YES, A QUITE APPROPRIATE ONE FOR THIS CASE, QUITE. IF YOU WILL INDULGE
THIS HUMBLE ONE IN SOMETHING OF A BOAST, FEW WHO HAVE EVER BECOME INVOLVED
NOW REMAIN—AND NONE BUT I HAVE VOLUNTARILY RE-INVOLVED MYSELF WHENEVER
WHEREVER THERE IS A REOCCURANCE. THIS DOES NOT OF COURSE MAKE ME ANY CLOSER
TO THE REAL BEGINNINGS OF IT THAN YOU.

STILL, WHEN ONE HAS SPENT SUCH TIME AND DEALT WITH THESE . . . YES, I SUPPOSE
YOU MAY CALL THEM INSCRUTABLE SUBTLETIES—ONE CAN BEGIN TO RECOGNIZE THE
CONSISTANCIES, THE PATTERNS, OR AS YOU CALL IT, THE MODUS OPERANDI.

PERMIT ME AN ILLUSTRATION—APPROPOS OF THIS CASE:
A PERSON APPEARS IN A PLACE FOR A LENGTH OF TIME, INTERACTING WITH OTHERS, AND
GOES—NOTHING UNUSUAL IN THAT . . . A PERSON APPEARS IN ANOTHER PLACE FOR
THE EXACT SAME LENGTH OF TIME, INTERACTING IDENTICALLY WITH THE SAME NUMBER
OF PEOPLE DOWN TO THE SMALLEST DETAILS—WHO CAN KNOW THAT ONE IS PART OF THE
OTHER? . . . WHO CAN RECOGNIZE THE SAME NAMES, THE SAME FACES, THE SAME
COURSE OF EVENTS? ONLY ONE WITH A VIEW OF SUFFICIENT BREADTH AND PATIENCE.

(2A IS A PARROT WHO MIMICS THE WORDS AND ACTIONS OF 2)
(DURING THE CHINAMAN'S SPEECH 3 SINGS A WORDLESS SONG, SUDDENLY—)

3   GET THEE BACK O CROCODILE THAT DWELLEST IN THE EAST

(1,2,2A SLAP AN IMAGINARY PERSON WITH GREAT FORCE)

1   GOOD DAY
2,2A   GOOD DAY

1   OK
2,2A   OK

(WHEN, IN THE SPEECH ON THE PRECEDING PAGE, THE CHINAMAN SAYS, "A PERSON AP-
PEARS," BILLY—"B."—THE GARDENER ENTERS, NOW AS AN OLD MAN.)

3   AND WHAT IS IT LIKE TO BE SO OLD
B.   I SIT IN THE SUN ON THE PORCH BECAUSE I LIKE THE WIND THERE

3   ONCE I WENT IN THE ARMY
B.   I WAS VERY YOUNG

3   ONCE I GOT A MEDAL FOR SHOOTING RIFLE
B.   EVERYONE IN THE UNIT HAD

3   THEN I CAME HOME WHEN THE MARCH WAS DONE
B.   THEN I TOOK WHITNEY IN MY LIFE

3   THEN SHE TOLD ME SHE HAD BEEN FRIGHTEN THAT DAY
B.   WE HAD SIX CHILDREN

3   WE ASK MOM FOR THEM
B.   AT THE END OF A LONG DAY AND YOU SIT AND REST FOR AWHILE AND WAIT FOR ANOTHER DAY

3   THEY ASK HOW IT WAS THEN
B.   IT WAS THE SAME

3   (LOW LOW VOICE) SO MANY MANY MANY MANY MANY

B.   SO MANY OF THE MEN OF THE VILLAGE GONE NOW ONLY I CAN REMEMBER

3   THE STREETS, MY HANDS MY HANDS
B.   MY FATHER SAILED A BOAT

3   JUST A LITTLE BOAT
B.   AND HE LAY BACK ON THE LITTLE BOAT AND LOOK AT THE SKY

3   I WORRY EVERY DAY WHEN HE WAS A BOY
B.   THEY GOT A GOOD DAY'S WORK OUT OF ME

3   I'M A MAN'S MAN
B.   ONLY ON SUNDAY DID SIT

3   SO MANY WORDS TO LISTEN TO AND MUSIC
B.   TWELVE OF US

3   HOW IS IT?
B.   IT'S IMMENSE

3   (SCREAM)

(SOUND OF BELLS SIMPLY AND CONSTANTLY FOR TWO MINUTES)

B.   NOTHING HAPPEN TO HER

3   NEVER MIND
B.   IT WAS MY FATHER-IN-LAW DO YOU REMEMBER

3   DO YOU REMEMBER THE TIME WE WENT SAILING
B.   I GUESS IT WAS KIND OF SMALL

3   SMALL?
B.   YES WE HAD TO LEAN OVER TO THE LEFT SIDE

3   THAT WAS REALLY FUN
B.   THEN WE BUILT A FIRE

3   AT NIGHT WE WARMED OURSELVES BY THE FIRE   (IT STARTS SNOWING)
B.   LOOK IT'S SNOWING (VERY TENDER)

                                                      (SOUND OF BELLS SOFTLY)
3   YEAH IT IS

(LIGHTS OUT)
(BILLY EXITS)
(LIGHTS UP)

(3 SINGS ARIA)

3 IT'S SEVEN O'CLOCK
   AND THE GENERAL'S NOT HERE YET
   HE MUST BE HAVING HIS SUPPER OR TARDY
   HE SAID HE'D MEET ME
   IN FRONT OF THE DRUGSTORE
   I BELIEVE HIM
   SO NOW I'M WAITING
   IMPATIENTLY FOR HIM TO COME
   I THOUGHT I HEARD
   SOMEONE KNOCKING AT THE DOOR!
   IT'S GETTING LATER AND
   LATER AND LATER
   HE'D BETTER COME PRETTY SOON
   OR I'LL SCREAM

(4 SCREAMS)

   AH!
   I WONDER WHAT EVER COULD BE KEEPING HIM?
   IT'S NOT AT ALL WHAT I'D EXPECT OF HIM
   WHO DOES HE THINK HE IS?
   I THINK I'LL JUST CALL MY LAWYER UP
   RIGHT AWAY
   BEFORE I TAKE A NAP ON THE SOFA HERE   (KNOCK KNOCK KNOCK)
   WHO'S THERE?
1 COME IN.   JUST A MINUTE.   BUT CAN YOU TELL US ANY MORE ABOUT IT   JE VEUX
   DIRE   I MEAN I THINK I'M WITH YOU. WE ARE RELATIVELY SURE THAT THERE WAS A
   CRASH, BUT THAT WAS A LONG TIME AGO. TELL ME SOMETHING MY FRIEND.   WHAT
   REALLY HAPPENED.   I MEAN YOU KNOW ME.
   I MEAN WHAT WHAT
           WHAT WHAT
           HAPPENED
           HAPPENED
           AT   A A
                 A A
           SEE A
           SEQUACHEE
           DA   A

(3 SLAPS BILLY)

(LIGHTS OUT)

ACT IV
SECTION 2

(LIGHTS UP)

2,2A   WE USE THOSE CRAFTY ORIENTAL TECHNIQUES YOU READ ABOUT
                                        TELEPHONE
                                        TELEGRAPH

3   NO BABY!
4   THEY APPRECIATE IT

1   YOU SAID YOU KNOW FRANK FOR TWENTY YEAR
2,2A   YOU SAID YOU KNOW BILL FOR TEN YEARS
3   HOW WELL DOES A SON KNOW HIS FATHER

(BILLY, THE GARDENER, REENTERS WITH HEDGE CLIPPERS)

4   IS THIS WHAT WE ARE LOOKING FOR

1   LET'S GET THINGS STRAIGHT
2,2A   IN TYWAN I'LL BE A POLICEMAN AGAIN
3   TELL ME ABOUT THE GANG HOW ARE THEY?

(2ND CHINAMAN ENTERS)
JULIA: BILLY BILLY
(CHINAMAN AND BILLY EXIT TOGETHER)

4   I DID NOT DO IT

1   HAVE SOME FAITH IN
2,2A   DON'T BOTHER I WON'T BE HERE   I'M SORRY DAD
3   YOU DON'T THINK THE KID IS GUILTY (LAUGH)
4   BILLY DID NOT

1   HOW CAN YOU EXPLAIN THAT
2,2A   I CAN'T
3   HOW ABOUT A POWERFUL FORCE STRIKING HIM FROM THE OPPOSITE DIRECTION
4   THE STREET SAYS IT WAS POSTED BY SOME OF THE BUSINESSMEN

1   NOT GUILTY? WHAT DID I DESERVE TO GET THIS?
2,2A   TALK WITH THE ELDERS
3   TAKE ME JUST AS I AM
4   WHAT WOULD YOU LIKE?

1   I THINK YOU HAVE A BOYFRIEND THAT'S IN SERIOUS TROUBLE
2,2A   WE HAD A COUPLE OF MORE COPS IN HERE LAST NIGHT
3   WHAT FOR?
4   WHAT DO YOU WANT

1	TO HELP BILLY IF I CAN
2,2A	DO WHAT YOU WANT
3	THERE MUST BE A WAY TO FIGHT
4	BUT WHAT ABOUT THE ATOM BOMB

1	AH HONEY
2,2A	I'M SORRY MARIA
3	COME MARIA
4	I KNOW

1	HOW CAN WE FIGHT SOMETHING WE DON'T SEE
2,2A	SCREAM
3	SCREAM
4	YOU'VE GOT TO SEE NOW

1	YEP IT'S BETTER
2,2A	COME ON
3	HELP YOURSELF
4	I WANT TO TALK WITH YOU ALONE

1	COME WITH ME
2,2A	WE HAVE WORK TO DO
3	HURRY PETE HURRY PETE (SOUND OF SCREAM)
4	I HOPE THE TRIP DOES WORK AGAINST US

1	I HOPE TO GO AROUND IT
2,2A	HERE PETE YOU HAVE A BETTER CHANCE WITH THIS (SCREAM)
3	IT'S GOING AWAY I'M GOING OUTSIDE
4	LOOK THERE

1	LET'S GET GOING
2,2A	FROM THE OUTER SIDE
3	YEAH
4	HERE HERE

1	YES
2,2A	WAIT THERE WAS A MAN WHO WAS HERE THAT SAID HE WAS EXPECTING YOU
3	IT'S ONE WAY SURPRISING MY BROTHER CLIFF
4	WELL SINCE I'M IN LONDON I SUPPOSE YOU KNOW THE REASON I'M HERE

1	THE ETERNAL YOUTH OF CHINA
2,2A	THINGS ARE GOING WELL?
3	I'M SURE I'LL LIKE IT HERE
4	I CAME TO BRING YOU A PRESENT

1	OH?
2,2A	DO YOU REALIZE WHAT YOU ARE GIVING ME?
3	YOU'RE A LUCKY FELLOW
4	MY GOODNESS I FEEL VERY AWKWARD ABOUT THIS

1   WELL PERHAPS THEY WERE TRYING TO KILL ME
2,2A   CHINA AND LOVE
3   THEY WON'T TRY AGAIN
4   YEAH SUE   THANK YOU   I FEEL INDEBTED TO YOU   YOU'RE MY BROTHER

1   YEAH AN EXCELLENT IDEA
2,2A   YES   (YELLED) HEY JIM
3   YOU DON'T EXPECT ME TO BE ENGLISH
4   YOU HAVE SAVED ME FROM A DESPERATE SITUATION

1   DO YOU MIND
2,2A   I NEVER KNOW IF YOU ARE SERIOUS OR NOT
3   THERE
4   SINCE WHEN DO YOU USE TOMATOES TO PLAY GOLF

1   PERHAPS
2,2A   HELLO MY FRIEND
3   THANK YOU
4   IT'S BEEN A PLEASURE FOR ME

1   AND FOR ME
2,2A   OH WELL I'M PLEASED THAT YOU CAME
3   IF YOU DON'T WANT TO TALK CHUM I JUST GOT A TELEGRAM FROM HONG KONG
4   (ANGRY) YOU ARE ABOUT TO HAVE ONE TOO MANY

1   DON'T BE DISTURBED
2,2A   PLEASE LEAVE ME ALONE
3   HE'S MY HALF-BROTHER   HIS MOTHER WAS CHINESE
4   COULD YOU POSSIBLY GET INTERESTED IN ME

1   YOU ARE SWEET   YOU ARE BECOMING IMPORTANT TO ME
2,2A   (SONG) THAT'S THE STOREE
3   SOMETIMES THESE TRACES
4   REMAIN HERE AND DON'T MOVE

1   REMAIN HERE I'LL BE RIGHT BACK
2,2A   LOOKING FOR ME
3   GET OUT HERE
4   CLIFF I'M FRIGHTEN

1   NOW WHAT WERE WE TALKING ABOUT
2,2A   YOU LIVE AN EXCITING LIFE MR. WREN
3   HM M M   HM M M
4   (SMALL LAUGH TO ONE'S SELF)

1   WHY ARE YOU HERE
2,2A   IT ATTACKED HER
3   WAS IT STRONG ENOUGH TO KILL A MAN
4   YOU WORK SO LONG TO FIND IT

```
2,2A   I'VE BEEN BAD AND FOOLISH
3      AND THIS IS WHAT YOU GET
4      WATCH OUT

1      HOW SILLY CAN YOU GET
2,2A   HERE YOU ARE
3      THERE'RE BOTH EXACTLY THE SAME
4      WAIT A SECOND

1      RACE AGAINST TIME
2,2A   OK HOW IS THAT?
3      WHAT ARE YOU GOING TO DO?
4      IT BROKE OUT OF THE BOX

1      WHAT YOU'RE SEEING IS REALLY HAPPENING
2,2A   GO WRONG   GO WRONG
       GO WRONG   GO WRONG
       GO WRONG   GO WRONG
3      DON'T HINDER ME   I'M THE GOVERNMENT'S AGENT
4      RESPONSIBILITY FROM HIS BODY KEPT HIM GOING ON

1      SCREAM SCREAM SCREAM SCREAM SCREAM FOR YOUR LIFE
                                              (4 SCREAMS)
2,2A   OK I'M SORRY I DID WHAT I
3      I KNEW SHE COULDN'T SCREAM
4      I GUESS THEY WILL ELECTROCUTE ME

1      AFTER YOU READ IT RETURN IT
2,2A   STOP THAT MUSIC
3      YOU SEE HE HAS NEVER KNOWN ANYONE EXCEPT SOMEONE LIKE HIS TAILOR
4      HOW SHOULD I KNOW THAT

1      SO NOW MY DEAR ALL I ASK YOU
2,2A   WHAT
3      I'M SORRY
4      ONE NEEDN'T BE

1      THE FIRST TIME YOU WERE ON STAGE YOU WERE LIKE ICE
2,2A   DON'T WORRY
3      REMEMBER WHAT I TOLD
4      REMEMBER WHAT I'VE TOLD YOU NOTHING MORE

1      I CAN WAIT I CAN WAIT ALL NIGHT
2,2A   TAKE YOUR TIME DON'T WORRY IF YOUR MIND GOES BLANK THEN LOOK AT ME

3      LIFE (THE GESTURE OF HAND DOWN, THEN I SINGS A SONG)
       WHEN MISSING IS YOURS WHO CARES
       WHO CARES
       IF MY ARMS WERE ONE
       THAT'S LIFE GOOD-BYE
```

```
4      MY SWEETHEART
1      (SUNG)
       NEAR ME
       KISS ME AND SAY THAT'S LOVE
       I'M YOURS
       WHO CARES
       LEAVE MY ARMS OUTSIDE
       THAT'S LIFE
       GOOD BYE


2,2A   I EXPECTED THIS
3      THE HONOR IS MINE
4      NOW TELL ME DID YOU LIKE THE PERFORMANCE


1      VERY WELL
2,2A   I CAN'T BELIEVE IT'S THE SAME ONE
3      MY ONLY LOVE
4      AH YES VERY NICE


1      HOW DARE SHE MAKE ME LOOK SO CHEAP
2,2A   YOU BETTER SAY GOODNIGHT WITH ME
3      OK
4      WHO ARE YOU


1      YOU SHOULD SAY THAT YET
2,2A   YES
3      WE WERE TRYING TO GET IN WE DIDN'T KNOW
4      YOU YOU EVER? HAVE YOU EVER? . . .


1      SOME OTHER NIGHT, YES?
2,2A   YOU GO
3      DARLING
4      VALUE CHARM


1      WHY DON'T YOU COME AND SEE
2,2A   GENTLEMEN GENTLEMEN
3      HI EVERYBODY I'M SHERYL
4      WE'RE SINGING IN THE TREE


1      FOUR RECORDS
2      IT TAKES 2 TO TANGO
3      PUT ONE OF THOSE RECORDS ON
4      GOOD MORNING HENRY   GOOD MORNING GEORGE


1      GOOD MORNING
2,2A   WHAT IS THE GARBLED FLY GEORGE
3      I'M SURE I DON'T KNOW
4      IT FLIES IN THE GARDEN
```

1   GEE, SHE DIDN'T IMPRESS ME THAT WAY AT ALL

4   (DELIVERED FAST) I'M NO WAY WELL THERE WE LET CRACK THE WHIP THEN WE
      OPERATE AT THE BASE I'LL SWEAR IT HI TOM NOW WHERE WERE YOU LAST FALL NOW
      ANYWAY IT WAS GETTING LATE—HE SAID WELL I KNOW IT WAS A GORGEOUS DAY HE
      WAS A GORGEOUS DAY AND HE SAID, "NOW SIR I DIDN'T" (WITH ENGLISH AC-
      CENT) (PAUSE)

      CRIME IS RIDING FASTER THAN EVER THIS IS AN EXCITING FIELD YOU CAN TRAIN NOW
      LET'S HAVE A LOOK AT A PAIR OF FROG'S LEGS THERE'S NOTHING EDIBLE ABOUT SO I
      RATHER NOT HAVE THEM AROUND BECAUSE IT IS INTERESTING THAT PEOPLE GET
      AWAY IN LIEU OF RABBIT LEGS IN OF FROG LEGS THERE ARE ONLY 20 SECONDS LEFT
      IT SOUND LIKE A YELLOW BELLY SAP SUCKER   WHY ARE YOU HIDING YOU WOULD BE
      NEEDED I'M PROUD OF YOUR RECORD BE 316117300 IT'S IMPORTANT INFORMATIONS
      IT WAS JUST A TRAINING STATION WE'LL NEED IT IT CERTAINLY IS TOP SECRET WE
      DON'T EVEN KNOW WHAT IT IS. CORRECT. YOU HAVE TO WORK YOUR WAY LAND
      MINDS OUR MISSION WILL BE EASIER VERY CLEARER. YOU JUST PRESS THIS LEVER TO
      ACTIVATE IT.   DESTROYER COMMAND.

                 2 DESTROYERS   3 DESTROYERS   4 4
                 2,2 DESTROYERS   3,3 DESTROYERS 4,4
                 2,4 DESTROYERS   3,3 DESTROYERS 4,4

4   NOW I'LL JUST REST FOR AWHILE LISTEN 99 RIGHT ON THE NOSE NUMBER 99 LAND
      MINDS. THIS IS A SERIOUS CHARGE!!!

      WELL I SEE THAT YOU ARE UP ON YOUR HISTORY THE NATIVE ARE VERY NERVOUS
      ABOUT IT EXCUSE US. IT'S IMPORTANT. WHY YES. OF COURSE YOU'IIEXCUSE ME I
      THINK IT WAS RATHER INDISCREET I OFTEN GO THERE OH YOU ARE HOPELESS KEEP ON
      TRYING NEXT TIME WILL BE A DIFFERENT STORY I WAS DISCONNECTED. WHAT'S UP.
      SEARCH ME WHEN I FLASHED ON THE LIGHTS THERE HE WAS I HAVE MY OWN THEORY.
      PLEASE YOU DON'T HAVE TO WORRY ABOUT ME I'M A MAN OF MY WORDS. YES. BY
      THE WAY PIN HIS EARS BACK. TRY NOT TO WORRY. HERE IS THE CLINCHING EVI-
      DENCE. I HATE THIS AS MUCH AS ANYONE. VERY WELL. MAY I ASK AN EXPLANATION.
      WOW! MR. MOBILE. MR. MOBILE I'VE GOT IT. COME ON. COME ON. GEE. DON'T
      FORGET YOU ASKED ME TO PLAY IT FOR YOU. THIS REALLY IS THE LAND OF A MILLION
      DANCES. THAT'S RIGHT. LISTEN. 26544, 44, 1000322 CHARGES FOR TAPE. WHAT DO
      YOU KNOW ABOUT DIAMONDS OF YOU DON'T MIND MIND WAITING. HAY. THEY HAVE
      NO CONFIDENCE IN US SO THAT ONE ACTUALLY BE A GREAT SUCCESS. YEAHA THAT'S
      RIGHT. WE CAN'T DO NOTHING ABOUT IT. IT'S NOT FOR ME TO SAY. WHAT'S IT ALL
      ABOUT? WHERE'S OTTO. HE'S SUPPOSE TO IN ON TODAY'S PLANE. IT'S DEFINITELY AN
      INSULT. COME ON LET'S. DO MIND TELLING US WHERE YOU'VE BEEN. LOOK! (POINT-
      ING)(SHOUT) LOOK OUT!
                 OK
                 OK
                 OK
                 GET—
      (SILENCE)   WILL YOU ALL RETURN PLEASE AT 8 O'CLOCK.

ACT IV
SECTION 3

1   STUFFY IN HERE
2,2A MORE ADRENALIN
3   SCREAM
4   YOU WERE HIS FRIEND

1   YOU CONVERTED ME INTO A INSTRUMENT
2,2A OF DEATH
3   BUT HOW?
4   YOU SHOCKED HIM

1   YOU REALLY SHOULD HAVE KICKED HIM TWICE
2,2A WHAT'S YOUR OPINION WE'D LIKE TO KNOW
3   SPUUUUT
4   WHAT'S IT ALL ABOUT (SING) THE FIRST TIME
                          MISSING PERSON

1   ANYTHING YOU SAY IT
2,2A I WAS CHECKING THE WOODS
3   WHAT'S WRONG
4   NOTHING

1   SHE'S A LITTLE SHY
2,2A SHE DID SEEM THREATEN CRY SOMETHING
3   WISH I COULD FIND TEN MORE JUST LIKE HER
4   WISH I COULD FINE ONE MORE JUST LIKE HER

4   ARE YOU LOOKING OR TRYING TO FORGET
1   HOW LONG AGO IS THIS?
2,2A IT DIDN'T FIGURE AT ALL BUT THERE IT WAS. WHAT'S ON YOUR MIND
3   WHAT'S THE BIT
4   THERE IS ALMOST NO ONE IS WANTS TO WORK THIS WAY

1   IT'S JUST NO ENOUGH INFORMATION FOR ME
2,2A NEXT WEEK ON 1974
3   WE WILL BE DISCUSSING THESE
4   BUT I DO REMEMBER THAT STILL

1   HAVEN'T SEEN YOU IN AGES
2,2A I WAS JUST WONDERING HOW YOU ADJUSTED
3   THIS IS NO REASON FOR WHAT'S BETWEEN US TO CHANGE
4   (LOUD) FOR CRYING OUT LOUD

1   OH IT WAS WONDERFUL
2,2A I DON'T WANT HER TO SEE YOU HERE
3   I MUST HAVE MISUNDERSTOOD
4   I DREW A LITTLE

1   NO WORK THIS HOUSE AND
2,2A   AND THE PEOPLE
3   THEY'RE SO DECEITFUL THEY DESERVE ANYTHING THAT HAPPENS TO THEM
4   WHAT DID YOU SAY ABOUT US NOT COMMUNICATING

1   WELL I'M GOING TO TELL YOU ABOUT IT
2,2A   MARK LET'S GO AWAY TOGETHER
3   MARK I LOVE YOU
4   I LOVE YOU TRUE

1   LOOK AT MY DRY SKIN
2,2A   YOU WHAT I LIKE ABOUT YOU BENNY? (ANGRY)
3   I CAN'T TELL YOU HOW THAT PLEASES ME   WHERE DID SHE GET THE INFORMATION
4   ALL RIGHT

1   THEN WHY DID GO TO BED A TELL FUNNY MOVIES
2,2A   KIDDING
3   REAL NO
4   I'LL DRINK TO THAT

1   HOW CAN YOU FIND ANYTHING
2,2A   YOU LIVE HERE
3   WELL YOU KNOW HOW IT IS
4   A LIBRARIAN 1928 SOUTHEAST KANSAS

1   STAY CLOSE IT LOOKS LIKE A NICE DAY. IT WON'T TAKE THAT LONG BEFORE WE SEE IT.
        HOW LONG WAS IT BEFORE YOU WIFE CHANGED HER ABILITY
2,2A   I'M NOT INTERESTED IN YOUR DEDUCTIONS, SHUT UP!
3   COME ON YOU HAVE NO WHERE TO GO (SUNG)
4   YES FORTUNATELY (SUNG)

1   I'LL MISS THE DESSERT
2,2A   I'LL UNDERSTAND
3   HELLO
4   HELLO

1   YOU BEEN AWAY
2,2A   WE PLAY GAMES
3   DO YOU WANT TO PLAY HIDE AND SEEK
4   OK COUNT 1 2 3 4 5 6 7 8 9 10   I WONDER WHERE HE COULD BE HIDING

1   HIS HAND HAS THE STROKE OF AN ADULT
2,2A   WE SHOULD TAKE ADVANTAGE OF OUR IGNORANCE
3   DO THAT
4   I THINK THAT'S A WAY OUT

1   I CAN ASSURE YOU I WON'T APPRECIATE IT
2,2A   I CAN ASSURE YOU THAT ISN'T MY MAJOR CONCERN I FIND THAT THAT'S IMPOSSI-
        BLE   S A K I T U M I (SPELL OUT) IT'S DONE IN MANY WAYS

3   OK MAYBE WE'RE GETTING SOMEWHERE—ON THAT POINT—JUST ON THAT POINT
4   (VERY FAST) 6987842324567

1   (VERY FAST) CHANEL 42321867
2,2A   (VERY FAST) YEAHA
3   ARE YOU OK?   SHE WAS HEADED STRAIGHT FOR THE JEWEL BOX ANYONE COULD SEE
       THAT
4   IT'S OVER HERE JIM

3   TAKE MY COUSIN MANDA SHE EVEN GOES IN DOORS BACKWARDS

4   YOU ARE LOOKING FOR THE GIRL YOU? YOU STICK AROUND

1   WHERE ARE WE GOING
2,2A   OUT OF HERE
3   IT'S NICE HERE ISN'T
4   YEAHA BEAUTIFUL

1   I USED TO PLAY HERE WHEN I WAS A KID
2,2A   YOU'RE A GARDEN LOVER I CAN SEE THAT (SUNG) MUSIC MAESTRO PLEASE

3   100004000   300   L C D 7 9,000
4   THAT'S ALL FORGET WHAT YOU HEARD   I COULDN'T MAKE UP MY MIND HAP HAT
       HATH HAT

1   OPEN THE DOOR MISS   I'VE BEEN LOOKING FOR YOU   THAT'S ALL THAT'S ALL   YOU
       MUST KNOW ALL THE REST   TAKE THE STONE AWAY   5 BILLION   YOU UNDERSTAND
       YOU UNDERSTAND   I WANT YOU JUST THE WAY YOU ARE   I'LL SEE YOU TOMOR-
       ROW   PEACEFUL DANDY

2,2A   BLOWING PERFUME IN THE AIR SOUTHEAST KANSAS 1928 MISS POLLY WHILE YOU ARE
       WAITING INDOOR SWIMMING POOL FALLING ON MY HEAD
3   (VERY LOUD) I'VE TOLD YOU WHERE TO GO SINCE I WAS 10 YEARS OLD. I WANTED TO
       TELL YOU WHERE TO GO NOW GET OUT OF HERE. YOU ARE THE KIND OF PERSON YOU
       ARE.

(3 TAKES JEWEL BOX FROM 4-CHINAMAN. BILLY ENTERS WITH GUN TAKES JEWEL BOX)

4   SHE ISN'T IN THERE   THE JEWEL BOX

1   WHERE IS THAT GOLD
2,2A   THEN TAKE US TO IT
3   I THOUGHT YOU DIDN'T KNOW ANYTHING ABOUT THE DOLPHIN
4   BILLY BILLY IS THIS THE END OF THE RAINBOW?
                         .
1   I'M COMING IN
2,2A   (SCREAM)
3   YOU MUST LISTEN TO ME STAND BACK

(BILLY SHOOTS 3 AND EXITS WITH JEWEL BOX)

1   MUSIC MAESTRO PLEASE   24   32   24
     12 12 12 34 33 33 34   24   32   24
     12 12 12 34 33 33 34   24   32   24
                            24   32   24

2,2A XXXXXXXXXXXXXXXXXXXXXXXXX
      XXXXXXXXXXXXXXXXXXXXXXXXX
      XXXXXXXXXXXXXXXXXXXXXXXX   WOOO (SOUND GET HIGHER)
3   GET UP AND GO   IF YOU ARE NOT THRILLED RETURN IT
4   OK

GEORGE: IT RAINED FOR 40 DAYS AND 40 NIGHTS AND WE HAVE TO START ALL OVER
          TONIGHT PLEASE PLEASE BABY BABY YEAHA SURE BABY MIGHT AS WELL DO
          SOMETHING WHY DON'T YOU TRY HOW ARE YOU DOING EVERYTHING IS GOING TO
          BE ALL RIGHT. COME ON IN COME ON IN. OK HERE I COME THEY TOLD ME I AM MY
          ADRENALIN IS FLOWING OH OH I SEE HEAVY CONTRACTION (BREATH HEAVY FAST
          CHOPPY) LOOKS FUNNY HUMH?HE'S OUT WITH THE CREW WORKING THE TELE-
          PHONE LINES. I'LL SAY ALL THE NICE WORDS TO YOU THAT YOU DESERVE. THE
          LAND IS HIGH HIGH AND THE WATER IS VERY LOW HERE. JIM I'M SURE WE CAN
          COUNT ON YOU YOU HAVE PLENTY OF TIME TO TAKE CARE OF IT

2,2A STOP! STOP! (LOUD)
3   CALL CONTROL RIGHT NOW

1   I'VE NEVER BEEN HERE BEFORE BEFORE THIS I'VE GOT E.E.G. IT'S GREAT TO BE PRETTY
      DOING PRETTY, PRETTY DIFFICULT PATTERNS TO OPERATE THAT TRAIN GOING
      AROUND THE TRACK. MY HANDS ARE RED AND ITCHY.
2,2A ALL RIGHT I'LL GET THE BOYS AND MARK THE AREA YOU HAVEN'T WASTED TIME   I AM
      TO BE YOU AND YOU ARE TO BE ME

(2 AND 2A SWITCH POSITIONS   2 IS NOW THE PARROT)

3   WE HAS TO BE READY
4   YEAH I GUESS SO. HOW INTRIGUING. YOU ARE BEGINNING TO TALK IN RIDDLES.

1   THERE ARE RIDDLES I DON'T TAKE MUCH NOTICE
2,2A BUT I WALKED I WALKED (OUT OF BREATH) WHO SAYS I HAVEN'T HAD TOO MUCH
      SUMMER. BECAUSE SOMETHING JUST PLAIN MEAN OUT. THAT'S THE STORY NO WE
      PRESS ON KEEP DIGGING THERE'S NO PRECISION HERE. BUT WE'RE ON TO SOMETHING
      KEEP GOING I TOLD HIM THAT THEY WERE TRYING TO SPEED UP HIS WORK VERY
      INDEED.

(MOVING SLIDE OF AIRPLANE UPSTAGE OF VENETIAN BLIND)

3   WE CAN'T AFFORD ANY MORE DELAYS. WOULDN'T IT BE FUNNY IF WE NEVER SAW
      THEM AGAIN
4   SOMETHING LIKE THAT I SUPPOSE

2,2A EXACTLY LIKE THAT WELL JUST SAY I'M NOT A DESIRABLE PROPERTY
3   I LOVE YOU   I LOVE YOU   I DON'T KNOW ANYTHING ABOUT YOU I PROMISED BY THE

WAY NEVER LET ANYONE CATCH YOU WALKING IN THE LIBRARY. SHE HAS SOMETHING SHE WANTS TO GIVE YOU SOMETHING. STAY WHERE YOU ARE.   (SCREAM)

4   STAY WHERE YOU ARE. (MUSIC ALONE) CUT IT OUT CRICKET. STAY RIGHT WHERE YOU ARE. THIS PLACE WILL REMAIN CLOSED FOR TONIGHT. I ARRIVED BY PLANE THIS AFTERNOON TRINIDAD BRAZIL MAYBE YOU WOULD BELIEVE ME. THERE MANDA GOT A DIVORCE. JIM DIDN'T KILL YOUR BROTHER AND I STILL THINK YOU ARE BETTER WAY BETTER WAY IS RUNNING THE RANCH. THIS IS YOUR ASSISTANT. HOW ARE DO YOU DO?   I HAVE NOT SEEN THIS.

1   OH I FORGOT YOU WOULDN'T TAKE ANYTHING FROM ANYONE WOULD YOU
2,2A YOU'RE RIGHT
3   SOMETIMES WE KNOW JUST WHAT YOU'RE THINKING. YOU KNOW YOU DON'T HAVE TO ANSWER ANY QUESTIONS. YOU DON'T HAVE TO DO ANYTHING . . . YOU JUST PUT YOUR LIPS TOGETHER AND BLOW. WHAT ARE YOU LOOKING AT ME LIKE THAT FOR. I DON'T WANT TO GET THE SHAKES. SUPPOSE SOMETHING HAPPENS.
4   I DON'T KNOW YOU. YOU INVITED ME ON THIS TRIP. LETS GET OUT OF HERE.
                                        (SOUND OF HELICOPTER
                                            OR MOTOR)
1   THIS JIM WHO IS IT?I DON'T UNDERSTAND WHAT KIND OF WAR WE ARE FIGHTING. WHAT IS IT?
2,2A I DON'T KNOW
3   SHUT UP. I COULD DO. LOTS OF PEOPLE HAVE SPENT TIME FIGURING THESE THINGS OUT—THEY KNOW MORE ABOUT IT THAN WE DO.
4   WHAT DO I DO TO KEEP MY SKIN LOOKING HEALTHY?

1   I GUESS IT JUST TRY TO KEEP YOU SKIN LOOKING HEALTHY. THAT WHAT IT'S ALL ABOUT.
2,2A SOMETIMES YOU MAKE ME SO MAD I COULD
3   WHY DON'T YOU PUT IT IN A GOLDFISH BOWL AND BE DONE WITH IT. I'LL REMEMBER, WHAT DO YOU WANT HERE? WAIT A MINUTE.

(3 CUTS BILLY'S THROAT)

4   HE'S NOT GOING TO RUN OUT ON US. YOU BETTER GET SOME SLEEP. NOTHING GOES WITH EVERYTHING.

1   WALK AROUND ME
2,2A THERE ARE NO STRINGS TIED TO ME
3   I'LL BE ALL RIGHT
4   KEEP OUT OF SIGHT

2A   IT'S A STOREE OF AN OLD MAN FROM THE LAND OF THE FREE IN OLD HONG KONG.   I NEED SOMEONE TO LOVE ME IN OLD HONG KONG.   I LEAVE HONG KONG FAR FROM ME BUT WHEN I TRIED TO LEAVE I NEED SOMEONE TO LOVE. THAT'S THE STORY OF THE THE WHO WAS ARRESTED IN OLD HONG KONG.

1   I'M ALWAYS FIGHTING. SUPPOSE I FAIL THEN I'M FRIGHTEN. IT MIGHT FAIL AND IF IT DOES AND, I DIE, THEN THERE IS SOMEONE ELSE. THERE WILL ALWAYS BE SOMEONE ELSE
2,2A YEAH

3   I HAVE A HUNCH THE WHOLE THINGS IS GOING TO BLOW UP. HAVE YOU EVER BEEN BIT
     BY A DEAD BEE? WHY DON'T YOU RUN AWAY?
4   AND LIVE ON A HAYSTACK

1   I'VE STAYED HERE JUST TO BE NEAR YOU
2,2A THE THE THE THE
     HEAVY EMOTION OF IT
     IT COMES OUT IN THE VERY UNDERSTATEMENT OF IT

(3 SHOOTS 4—THE CHINAMAN)

(BREAK DROP DOWN)

(ROBERT WILSON IN FRONT OF LIGHT BREAK DROP OF DAM. HE SCRATCHES HEAD.)

BOB: PIRUP

ACT IV
SECTION 4

(BREAK DROP)

(4 BECOMES 2 FROM ACT I. 3 BECOMES 1 FROM ACT I.)
(PILOTS REENTER)

PILOTS: I DON'T KNOW HOW TO THANK YOU
             (PAUSE 5 SECONDS)
         SAY
             (PAUSE 4 SECONDS)
         WHAT
             (PAUSE 3 SECONDS)
         CERTAINLY
3   MY KNOWLEDGE ABOUT YOU IS REDUCED TO A HANDFUL OF FACTS

(PILOTS EXIT)

1 AND 2 ALTERNATE   SEEM WHAT
                     SEEMED WHAT
                     SEEM
                     SEEMS THE SAME
                     SEEMED THE SAME
                     SEEMS
                     SIMULTANEOUSITY O'CITY O'VORST
                     WHEEL WHAT WHEN NOW
                     AN ALLIGATOR'S SPAN
                     SEEM WHY
                     SEEM WHAT
                     SEEMED

```
SEEMS
SCREEN TELL A VISIONS
SCREENED TOLDA VISIONS
SCREEN
SCREAM
A MILLION DANCES
```

(FRAMED IN WHITE LIGHT)

A	HAP HAT HAP	AAAAAAAAAAAAO	CONFORMING	0
AO	HATH HIP HA	AAAAOAOAOA	VCONFORMIN	OK
OAOA	HAT HIT HAP	AAAOAOAOA	VECONFORMI	AOKO
XXXXX	HATH HAP HA	AAOAOAO	VERCONFORM	LAOKOK
AOAOAOA	HIP HIT HATH	AOAOA	VERYCONFOR	LLAOKOKO
XXXXXXXXX	HAP HATH HI	OAO	VERYVCONFO	ELLAOKOKOK
XXXXXXXXXXX	HAP HI HATH	AO	VERYVECONF	WELLAOKOKOK
OAOAOAOAOAOAO	HI HI HAP HA	0	VERYVERCON	AWELLAOKOKOKO

A BIT

A

LITTLE BIT

A

THE PILOT TILTS

A   SLANTING   PILOT   TILTS

A

AROUND   A   LITTLE   BIT

THE   ANGLE   OF   THE   THING   ANGLING

(1 AND 2 SCREAM SONG)

(CURTAIN)

THE RED HORSE ANIMATION
LEE BREUER

LEE BREUER:
MABOU MINES

Mabou Mines is the only group represented here that is concerned with the development of acting skills and story telling techniques. In *The Red Horse Animation*, a collaborative creation, the actors integrate motivational (internal) techniques, Grotowskian body expression and Brechtian commentary (external) techniques to provide a synthesis in which space is emotionalized in a series of non-sequential stage pictures. Structured as a choral narrative, the piece compels the actors to speak *out* rather than speak *to* one another. Dialogue gives way to an interior monologue which involves the actors in the emotional life of the Horse. Simultaneously they form images of the Horse and narrate his life story. In this way, the actors document events that have happened in the past, at the same time feeling the Horse's emotions, and using their bodies in a poetic affirmation of the Horse.

Red Horse unfolds in a bare floor space, backed by a wood-slatted wall; contact microphones underneath the specially designed space cause it to function as a percussion instrument (as when the actors tap on the floor for the sound of the Horse's galloping). The actors use both the back wall and the floor space—together they form a ninety-degree angle performing space. The floor space serves as a performance area in which they interact for the most part horizontally (i.e., lying down on the floor) rather than vertically (i.e., standing up—which is the more conventional mode of performing). This is one of the most radical uses of performance space to be seen up to this time in the American theatre. It is a major aesthetic breakthrough and changes the viewing relationship of the audience to the image by shifting the plane of reference from vertical to horizontal. This redefinition of performance space necessarily forces the audience, whose optimum seating angle is forty-five degrees from the stage floor, to view the action from above—a vast departure from normal sight lines. On this plane, defined as a huge canvas by the actors' horizontal (flat) interactions, a series of images are enacted that enliven the poetic text of *Red Horse*. Similar reorganizations of stage space have been seen before in dance performance but not in the theatre.

Unfortunately, theatre has been slow to redefine space and movement primarily because of the traditional need for theatrical performance to serve as an illustration of the dramatic narrative. Historically, American theatre has favored realism, unlike European theatre which has placed greater emphasis on textual and directorial experimentation. The building of non-proscenium theatres helped to remedy the situation somewhat as did the playwrights of the sixties. But the major challenge came with The Living Theatre, The Open Theater, the Happenings movement and, more recently, the environmental theatre experiments of The Performance Group. These groups defied conventional uses of space and text, with the result that the rigidity of theatrical practice broke down, performance values gained ascendency over dialogue, and the visual image began to supplant language in the hierarchy of theatrical elements. The actor's body was freed to function in a setting designed with new spatial concepts in mind. The text more often than not served as a basis for verbal-visual collage.

A generation ago Merce Cunningham modernized the dance by freeing it from exclusively reinforcing musical mood and story. All the elements of the dance performance could function autonomously once the narrative form was discarded. Dances were personalized—they could be about themselves. Similarly, *Red Horse,* which suggests dance in its choreographic use of rhythm and movement, is as much about the creative process as it is about the life of a horse.

If *Red Horse* shows the influence of modern dance, it also has roots in modern painting. The flat (painterly) perspective of the performance replicates, in so far as theatre can, the sense of an "action painting." Lee Breuer's theatrical mode of conceiving the piece links him in spirit and technique with the abstract expressionists who offered content on an emotionally charged plane (canvas) which, in turn, emphasized the process of creation. In the performance of *Red Horse,* three actors develop a series of choral narratives which pictorialize both anthropomorphic and abstract images of the Horse as he experiences life or recollects his past. At the end of the performance his image disintegrates into space. At times two actors portray the Horse while another serves as his rider; elsewhere, the image breaks apart into three separate figures scattered about the stage as if the Horse were melting in space. These transformations of the actors—their creation of shifting realities in rapid succession—make the performance appear spontaneous rather than planned, by focusing on momentary experience. The transformations also suggest a cubist perspective—the notion of seeing more than one side of an object or figure in space—which reflects multiple aspects of the Horse's inner life in the interplay of words and images. The body of the actor is used sculpturally: It is a medium for transporting the Horse's feelings through successive images that quickly dissolve and give way to other poses.

In *Red Horse* images correspond directly or indirectly to the language of the text. Thus, when the actors repeat, "I go through my changes . . . Forwards and Backwards," the Horse image reverses position. Sometimes a side view is offered or a rider will change places with another actor who had functioned as part of the Horse. The effect is that of a kinetic sculpture. The actors do not remain sculptural figures in a predetermined volume of space, but act as kinetic forms which continually reorganize it. They outline areas of space in which an image (the Horse) creates a kind of spatial poetry—a poetry-in-motion. The Horse describes his experiences under headings like Roman numerals, Arabic numbers and capital letters (the formal "Outline"). The actors' opening lines are "The Red Horse. The Animation of an Outline." That the Horse slips at one point from Roman Numeral II to IV points to the elliptical structure of the piece: It is only possible to glimpse scenes from the life of the Horse. This partial view is ironically reinforced by an actor pinning photographs of the Horse on the back wall of the stage space, as if to construct a photo album. At the same time, it emphasizes the theatricality of *Red Horse* by juxtaposing concrete images of the Horse with the metaphorical images of the actors.

Breuer took many of the horse images from Edweard Muybridge's *Animals in Motion,* a pioneering photographic study which shows horses galloping, trotting, cantering, etc. Breuer, in fact, rehearsed his actors using many of the sequences. What he has done in this piece is to activate the horse image, adding an interior monologue which conveys the animal's existential musings—his consciousness of himself. *The Red Horse Animation* is a fable in which the Horse expresses his feelings about identity, his sense of time and space and an awareness of nature in a fragmented narrative that disregards temporal and spatial order. Recollections of childhood, sorrow at the death of a father, joyous communion with nature are recast in visual puns, sight gags and concrete and abstract images in order to complete the composition of the "action painting."

Many of the images are spatial. The words "form," "shape," "circles" and "lines" are repeated again and again in the text as if the Horse were aware of his exact position in space. This physicality of the text is duplicated in the actors' rigorous body movements: spinning, acrobatic falls, turning and rolling over. Their constant convolutions in space offer a kaleidescopic perspective which often throws the actors into relief.

When the Horse's father Daily Bread (signifying both money and sustenance) is choked to death in a fatal leap, the actors "leap" up onto the back wall of the performing space. When the Horse reminisces about the past, the actors lie on their backs, each with one foot in the air; as a stationary image, moving their legs at a comfortable "trot," the actors show the Horse contemplating near a stream. Because of the unique combination of internal and external acting techniques the actors never become the animal in the conventional sense of creating character; they are merely a metaphor for the Horse, commenting on his life while feeling his true emotion.

"Do I owe a debt to the cinema?" asks the Horse—a question that is as operative as it is humorous. It functions both as a comment on the influence of cinema in the work, and the self-conscious reflection of Breuer. The sudden voicing of "Cut"—one actor says, "Eleven Seven. Genghis Khan institutes the craft of delivery by horse. Cut. Pan of the Gobi Desert. Cut."—interrupts the stage picture. This stop in time serves to frame the image in tableau while creating the impression of a still photograph. Dissolves of images from one scene to another, the overlapping of images in a tripartite form and the fade-outs at the end of a scene bleed the contours of time and space, suggesting the filmic "frame" as an important unit of composition. Furthermore, in performance, the work gives the impression that its director edited "in the camera" as it were, particularly in its rapid transitions, easy relationships between images, and seams-showing quality.

If *Red Horse* owes a debt to movie-making it pays homage more directly to another "popular" form, the comic book. The use of the comic book form to document a performance is nothing short of a radical departure from theatrical convention. It means simply that the dramatic form, as we have traditionally known it, is entirely inadequate to convey the sense of performance. Essentially, Breuer's non-dramatic attitude, i.e., his disdain of conventional dramatic form, has led him to create (with designer Ann Elizabeth Horton) a second art form as a radical textual alternative. The comic book uses both painterly and lithographic techniques in a design derived from the stage production. Substituted for the conventional play script are thirty-two individual color plates which "quote" scenes from the actual performance of *Red Horse*, alternately showing the actors as they appear in performance, and the Horse himself. Thus, two images are used: an anthropomorphic one and one based on reality. The reader must then make the sophisticated transfer from the metaphorical to the actual, a process that is very personal and *not* a passive reading experience.

As a montage of words and images, the comic book situates its meaning somewhere between image and caption. Since the two together provide the narrative framework of *Red Horse,* the risk of misinterpreting the visual counterpart of the story is much less than exists, for example, with a captioned photograph. The text verbalizes images and the images pictorialize the language of the script. For the reader in this age of multi-media it provides a dual experience: instant picture accompanied by a running commentary.

Long ago the silent film discovered the viability of a picture accompanied by a verbal narrative that would relate to it contrapuntally. In contemporary cinema Godard's films best exemplify this dialectic which serves as the basis of his arrangement of text and image. And in photography Duane Michals has coordinated text and image by exhibiting his sequential photographs coupled with a commentary that is more narrative than caption.

The comic book form, historically considered a "low" art form, is given by Breuer a literary reality. Paradoxically, at the theatrical level, *Red Horse* remains non-literary because it is primarily imagistic. Breuer's act is a sociological statement on "high" and "low" cultural prejudices and offers a transvaluation of comics as well. He offers a serious commentary as a fable for adults, in a form usually enjoyed only by young people.

Breuer follows in the American avant-garde tradition of using "popular" art forms in serious art. (Foreman and Wilson have used a variety of "popular" forms, including melodrama, television, film and music.) He has gone beyond Michael McClure's purely literary use of comics. And, unlike pop artists Andy Warhol and Roy Lichtenstein who playfully or critically have used comic strip techniques in their painting, Breuer stands outside the pop art school by virtue of the context in which he defines his animations. He does not use the comic form to signify an idea or attitude—critical or nostalgic—as pop artists usually do, but as an end in itself, its own art form. Moreover, Breuer and Horton have given the form metaphysical content in addition to extending its formal capabilities.

Red Horse is a comic poem which unashamedly appropriates all the conventions of comics: cuts, bubbles, overlapping, voice-overs and voice-offs, narrative boxes, dark print. For Breuer *Red Horse* is his very own "caption literature"—his term for this radical alternative to drama which serves as the formal document of a work conceived for the stage.

BONNIE MARRANCA

David Warrilow, JoAnne Akalaitis, Ruth Maleczech.   Photo © Babette Mangolte.

PREFACE:

LEE BREUER

I TRY TO GET DOWN TO JUST WHY I GET OFF ON COMICS • I'M NOT A COLLECTOR
• I COULDN'T NAME BATMAN'S INKER IN 1951 • BUT COMICS TALK TO ME •
MORE PERTINENTLY NOW • EVEN • THAN THEN • WHEN I WAS THE GREEN
ARROW • (WINNER NORTH HOLLYWOOD PARK HALLOWEEN COSTUME COMPETI-
TION 9 P.M. IN FRONT OF THE BONFIRE OCTOBER 31, 1948) • THEY TALK TO ME
AT ALL HOURS • ON THE PHONE • LONG DISTANCE.

I WALK AROUND IN A SQUARE BLACK FRAME • MY FIGHTS GO OFF THE PAGE • I
OBSERVE IN INSERTS • I COME ON IN CLOSEUP • WHEN I TALK TO MYSELF THE
IMPORTANT WORDS ARE SET OFF IN BLACK FACE TYPE • DRAMATIC MOVEMENTS
HAVE "POW" "KRACK" AND "AARGHH" WRITTEN ALL OVER THEM • I FLY • I
TAKE BATHS IN HEROIC POSES • AND FEAR CONSTANTLY FOR MY SECRET IDEN-
TITY • MY SCENE • SET IN YELLOW BOX UPPER LEFT OF THE TITLE PAGE • IS A
CROSS BETWEEN PHYSICAL KITCH • MENTAL PULP • AND SPIRITUAL TRUE
ROMANCE • MY COVER IS BY JIM APARO • "THE END" WILL BE SCRIPTED •
RIGHT ON MY SOD • AND BENEATH IN CAPITALS "CONTINUED NEXT WEEK!"
"WATCH FOR IT!" •

LEE BREUER

PREFACE:

ANN ELIZABETH HORTON

GIRL 11, UNDAUNTED BY FALL FROM HORSE

. . . The horse shied from the boulder and I fell off hitting the rock and losing consciousness—for a month I explored detail from my bed. Learning to walk again I was swept away. But for a time in my childhood I was allowed to pause in stillness. All that is real and of my dreams is connected with the pictures in my horse books.

Approaching the *Red Horse*, I opened those books again.

I began my journey buried in sand—later, riding, I saw the boulders. Suddenly the wind hit my face as I rode the Mongol horse into *terra incognita*. The vast desert space was a sign of regeneration, and I sped on. I gained nourishment as in ancient times a rider lived by the blood his horse gave.

The *Red Horse* is celebration.

ANN ELIZABETH HORTON

120

A CUT FROM
THE RED HORSE ANIMATION

IN THE DAYS OF GENGHIS KHAN RED HORSES WERE RESERVED FOR SPECIAL
JOURNEYS • THEY CARRIED MESSAGES WRAPPED AROUND ARROWS TO INDICATE
POSTE HASTE • THEY SPENT THEIR LIVES CROSSING THE GOBI DESERT •
WHIPPED CRAZY • STATION TO STATION • THEN HOBBLED • SAY • MONTHS •
WAITING • WHILE THE MESSAGE THEY HAD CARRIED WAS RELAYED ON • EACH
LIFE • SAY EACH CROSSING • ONE HORSE CARRIED FOUR HUNDRED DIFFERENT
MESSAGES EACH ONE FOUR HUNDREDTH OF THE WAY • CARRIED SAY "VICTORY
IS OURS" OVER THE CHOWRINGHEE ROCK BASIN • THEN "ALL IS LOST" • THE
RED HORSE CARRIES "ALL IS LOST" IN SNOW IN CIRCLES • SAY • IN THE MIDDLE
OF ITS PASSAGE WOULD NOT SAID HORSE BECOME CONFUSED ABOUT THE TRUTH
OF WHAT IT WAS CONVEYING • WOULD IT NOT CRAVE A CONSTANT PIECE OF
INFORMATION TO DELIVER • SAY FOR DELIVERANCE • COULD NOT IT THEN
PERCEIVE ITS GOING AS ITS BEING • IN THE DESERT • SAY GOBI DESERT •
COULD IT NOT DELIVER THEN ITS MOTION • WRAPPED AROUND AN ARROW • SAY
ITS DANCE •

MABOU MINES opened a first version of *The Red Horse Animation* at the Guggenheim Museum on November 18, 1970. The production was later revised and expanded for a presentation on April 22, 1972 at the Whitney Museum. Lee Breuer wrote, directed and designed the piece.

Cast .... JoAnne Akalaitis, Ruth Maleczech,
David Warrilow
Music .... Philip Glass
Color Photography .... Peter Moore
Lighting .... Jene Highstein
Wrestling Mat .... Tina Girouard

Rehearsals for *The Red Horse Animation* were subsidized in part by the LaMama Experimental Theatre Club.

A conventional script of *The Red Horse Animation* does not exist. The comic book published here, with story by Lee Breuer and art by Ann Elizabeth Horton, was taken from the stage production by MABOU MINES.

THE RED
HORSE ANIMATION

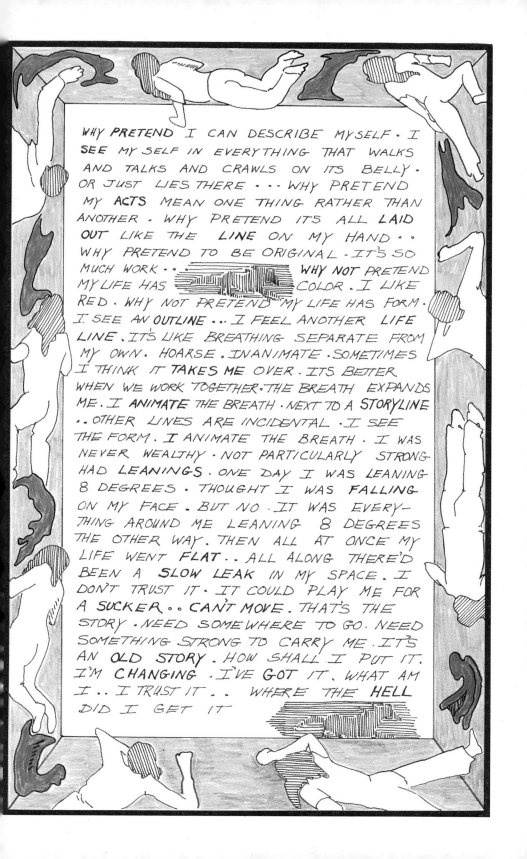

WHY **PRETEND** I CAN DESCRIBE MYSELF. I **SEE** MY SELF IN EVERYTHING THAT WALKS AND TALKS AND CRAWLS ON ITS BELLY. OR JUST LIES THERE ... WHY PRETEND MY **ACTS** MEAN ONE THING RATHER THAN ANOTHER. WHY PRETEND ITS ALL **LAID OUT** LIKE THE **LINE** ON MY HAND .. WHY PRETEND TO BE ORIGINAL. IT'S SO MUCH WORK ... **WHY NOT** PRETEND MY LIFE HAS COLOR. I LIKE RED. WHY NOT PRETEND MY LIFE HAS FORM. I SEE AN **OUTLINE** ... I FEEL ANOTHER LIFE LINE. IT'S LIKE BREATHING SEPARATE FROM MY OWN. HOARSE. INANIMATE. SOMETIMES I THINK IT **TAKES ME** OVER. ITS BETTER WHEN WE WORK TOGETHER. THE BREATH EXPANDS ME. I **ANIMATE** THE BREATH. NEXT TO A **STORYLINE** .. OTHER LINES ARE INCIDENTAL. I SEE THE FORM. I ANIMATE THE BREATH. I WAS NEVER WEALTHY. NOT PARTICULARLY STRONG HAD **LEANINGS**. ONE DAY I WAS LEANING 8 DEGREES. THOUGHT I WAS **FALLING** ON MY FACE. BUT NO. IT WAS EVERY-THING AROUND ME LEANING 8 DEGREES THE OTHER WAY. THEN ALL AT ONCE MY LIFE WENT **FLAT** .. ALL ALONG THERE'D BEEN A **SLOW LEAK** IN MY SPACE. I DON'T TRUST IT. IT COULD PLAY ME FOR A **SUCKER** .. CAN'T MOVE. THAT'S THE STORY. NEED SOMEWHERE TO GO. NEED SOMETHING STRONG TO CARRY ME. IT'S AN **OLD STORY**. HOW SHALL I PUT IT. I'M **CHANGING**. I'VE **GOT** IT. WHAT AM I .. I TRUST IT .. WHERE THE **HELL** DID I GET IT

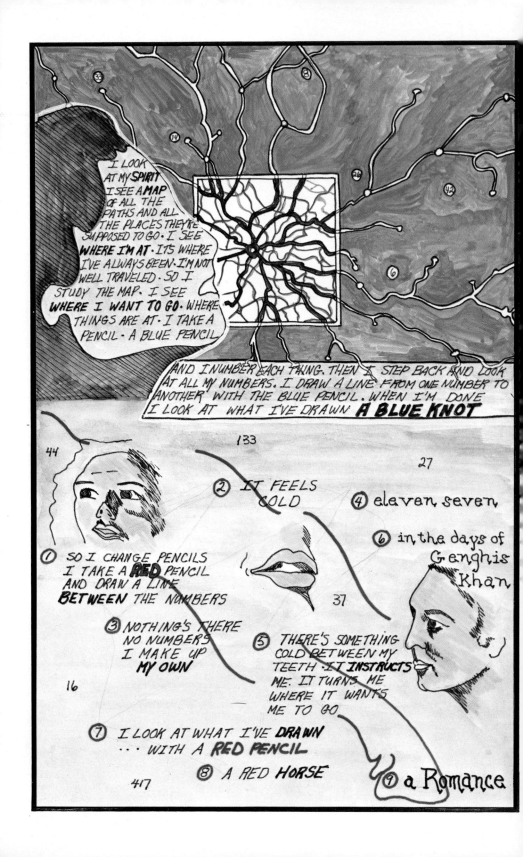

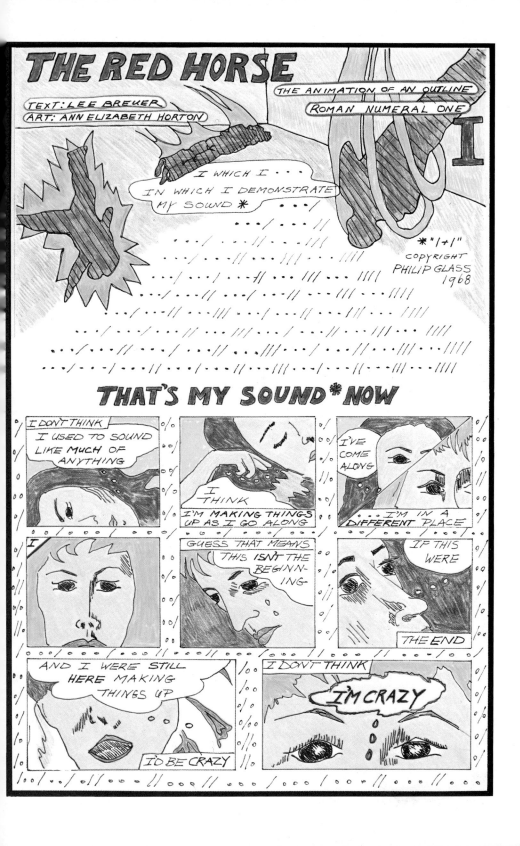

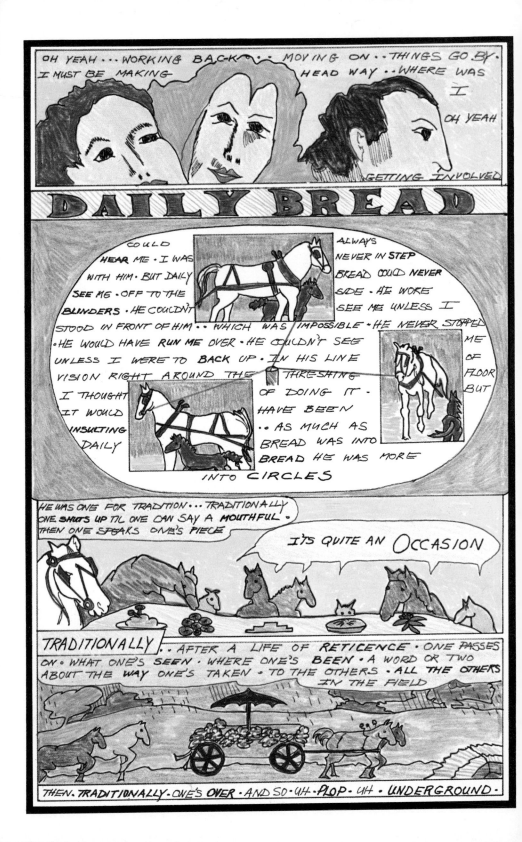

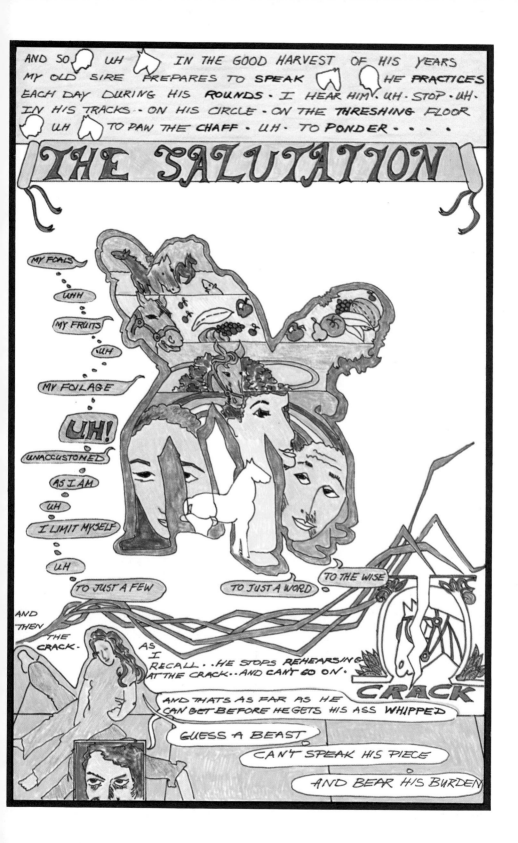

HOW IN MID-AIR IT

CRACKED HIS WIND-PIPE

HOW HE SPOKE THEN

FREELY

WHO HE WAS SPEAKING TO

ME

NO OTHERS IN THE FIELD

HOW I COULDN'T UNDERSTAND A WORD HE WAS SAYING · WITH HIS WINDPIPE CRACKED HE COULDN'T

MAKE A SOUND

THE WAY HE CONCLUDED · AND WAITED · ON ONE KNEE · DAILY BREAD WHAT COULD YOU HAVE BEEN WAITING FOR...

· · · APPLAUSE I'LL BET · · ·

HE WAS FULL OF THAT **HORSE SHIT**

A YELLOW **STAR** APPEARED · · · TIP OF HIS TONGUE WHERE THE WISE WORDS WERE · THAT SHOULD HAVE BEEN **MINE** · · TRADITIONALLY · THEY WERE STILL **IN HIS MOUTH** · · I · COULD TELL ·

THE TONGUE WAS GOLDEN

I BIT IT OUT · · ·

FADE

AND HAVING LEARNED NOTHING ABOUT **CIRCLES** ·

· · · I STARTED **RUNNING**

V
treble clef
voices
etc.
etc.
plus
percussion
etc.
etc.
etc.
etc.
etc.
etc.

"Music for The Red Horse Animation"
copyright Phil Glass 1971

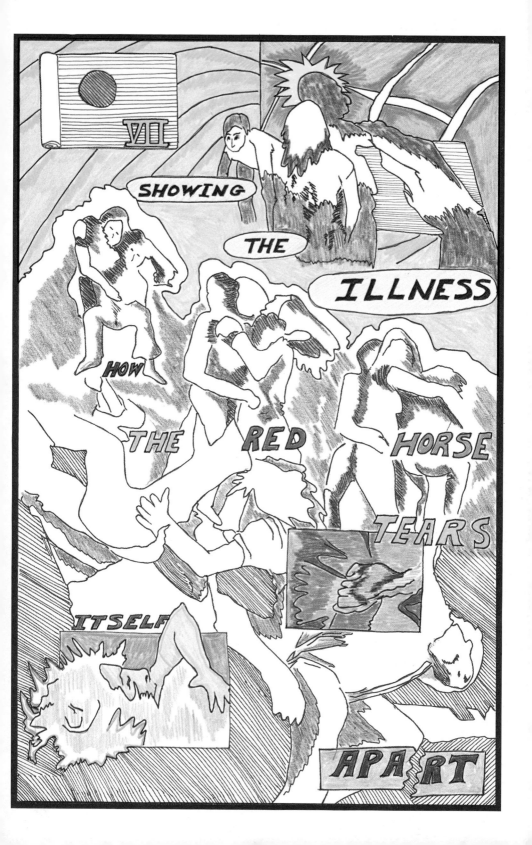

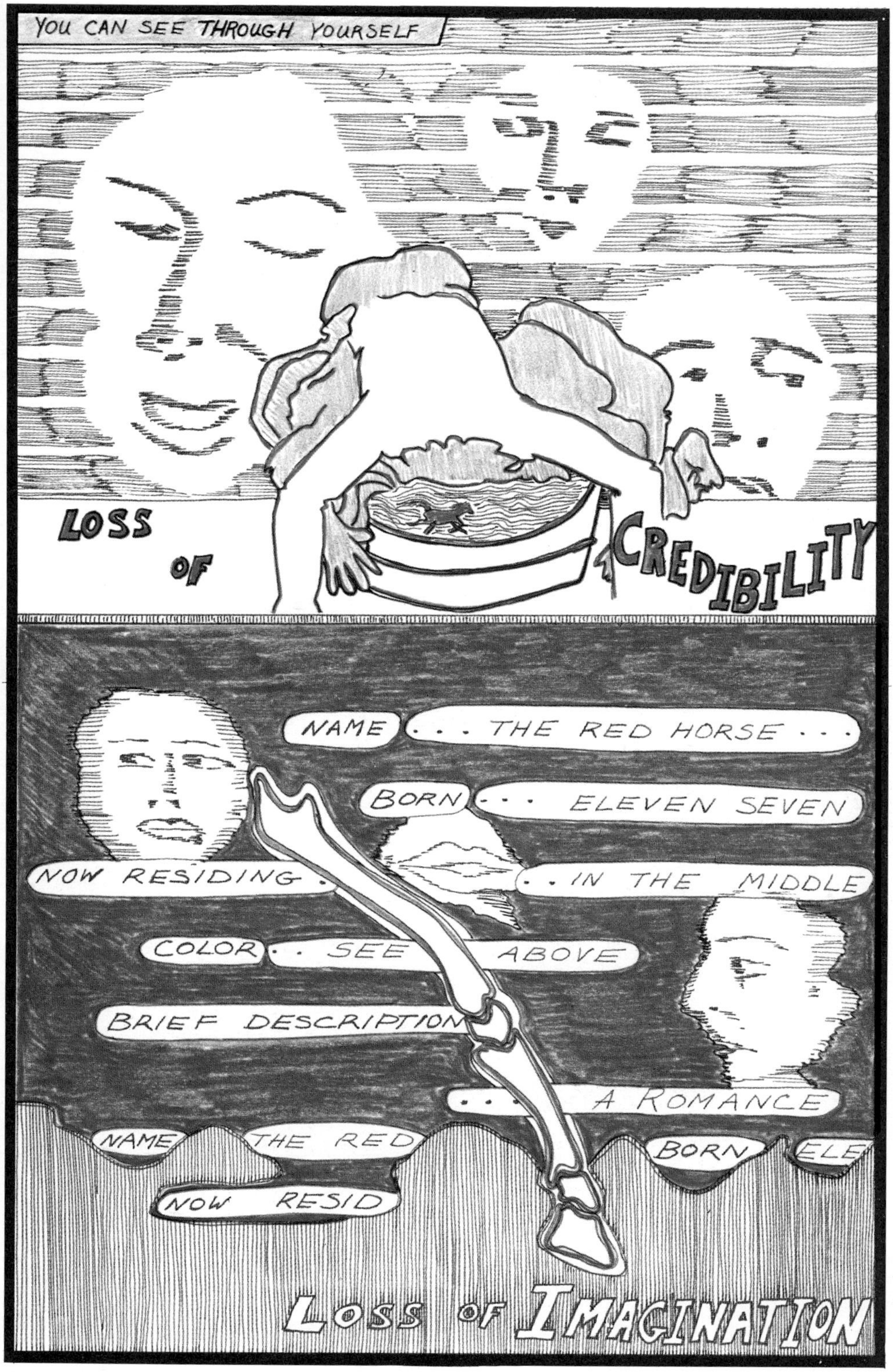
YOU CAN SEE THROUGH YOURSELF
LOSS OF CREDIBILITY
NAME . . . THE RED HORSE . . .
BORN . . . ELEVEN SEVEN
NOW RESIDING . . . IN THE MIDDLE
COLOR . . SEE ABOVE
BRIEF DESCRIPTION
. . . A ROMANCE
NAME THE RED
BORN ELE
NOW RESID
LOSS OF IMAGINATION

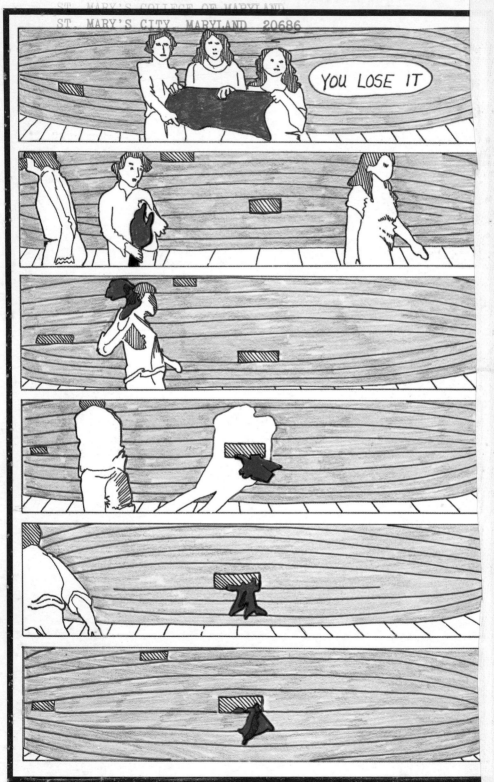